HOWARD HENDRICKS

BOB PHILLIPS

MULTNOMAH BOOKS ❦ SISTERS, OREGON

VALUES AND VIRTUES

published by Multnomah Books
a part of the Questar publishing family

© 1997 by Howard Hendricks and Bob Phillips

International Standard Book Number: 1-57673-086-7

Edited by Candace McMahan
Cover photo illustration by: Mike Radencich
Cover design by: Kevin Keller

Printed in the United States of America

For information:
QUESTAR PUBLISHERS, INC.
POST OFFICE BOX 1720
SISTERS, OREGON 97759

Library of Congress Cataloging--in--Publication Data
Values & virtues/[compiled] by Howard G. Hendricks & Bob Phillips.
p.cm.   ISBN 1-57673-086-7 (alk. paper)   1. Quotations, English. 2. Wit and humor.
I. Hendricks, Howard G. II. Phillips, Bob. 1940

PN6081.V35   1997   96-49714
082-dc21   CIP

97 98 99 00 01 02 03 04 — 10 9 8 7 6 5 4 3 2 1

CONTENTS

INTRODUCTION

If you find a wise sentence or apt phrase,
commit it to your memory.

HENRY SIDNEY

The wisdom of the wise and the experience of the ages are
perpetuated by quotations.

BENJAMIN DISRAELI

I quote others only in order the better to express myself.

MICHEL DE MONTAIGNE

King Solomon said,
"A man has joy in an apt answer, and
how delightful is a timely word!"

PROVERBS 15:23.

He went on to say, "Like apples of gold in settings of silver
is a word spoken in right circumstances."

PROVERBS 25:11

Through centuries of recorded human history, the common man has enjoyed and utilized proverbs, epigrams, and homey phrases to describe the experiences of everyday life. Proverbs enable thoughts to be communicated and exchanged without a great deal of effort.

It was said of King Solomon that he had committed to memory three thousand proverbs. Aristotle, Cicero, Plutarch, and Cato the Elder were creators and collectors of pithy phrases and tidbits of truth. Today, libraries and bookstores are filled with delightful and stimulating books of quotations.

Following the tradition of those who love to collect quotable quotes and salty sayings, we found that putting together *Values and Virtues* was a labor of love and joy. This collection, gathered during decades of speaking and writing, contains most of our favorites and ranges from classical wisdom to simple folk sayings. Since profound thoughts often are brilliantly expressed in a few short words or sentences, we have frequently caught ourselves smiling or nodding in agreement at these down-to-earth insights into human nature.

This book contains more than two thousand quotations divided into thirty values and virtues. We identified the author of each quotation when possible. The individuals to whom we have attributed these quotations may not have been the first to make these statements, but over time the statements have been attributed to them, and the names of the true originators have been lost. The originators of many, if not most, brief quotes and proverbs are impossible to identify.

You'll find *Values and Virtues* a treasure chest of wise and witty sayings that can add sparkle to your speech and can challenge you to a life of moral excellence. It is not only an entertaining fireside read, but also a rich resource for public speakers, authors, pastors, Sunday school teachers, Bible study leaders, school teachers, youth leaders, counselors, camp directors. You can refer to these gems when guiding and advising your children. Use them in newsletters or church bulletins. Add a pertinent quotation at the start or end of a letter. Share a quote or two over the phone with a friend. Better yet, share the entire volume—we've designed the book so that it can serve as a fine gift for family, friends, business acquaintances.

We hope you enjoy this rich heritage of wit and wisdom of the ages. As you read these thoughts, we pray that the practical advice will stimulate and challenge you. We encourage you to share these thoughts with others. Remember, you only keep what you give away. As you pass on values and virtues, they will enrich your own lifestyle and character as they minister to those around you.

HOWARD HENDRICKS
BOB PHILLIPS

ACHIEVEMENT

Three great essentials to achieve
anything worthwhile are,
first, hard work;
second, stick-to-itiveness;
third, common sense.

THOMAS EDISON

What one has to do usually can be done.

A good rooster crows in any henhouse.

ELEANOR ROOSEVELT

Those who dare to fail miserably can achieve greatly.

ROBERT F. KENNEDY

My most brilliant achievement was my ability to persuade my
wife to marry me.

WINSTON CHURCHILL

He who would accomplish little must sacrifice little; he who
would achieve much must sacrifice much.

JAMES ALLEN

He who boasts of his accomplishments will reap ridicule.

Actions speak louder than words—but not so often.

FARMERS' ALMANAC

When we have fully discovered the scientific laws that govern
life, we shall realize that the one person who has more
illusions than the dreamer is the man of action.

OSCAR WILDE

8

The only measure of what you believe is what you do.
If you want to know what people believe, don't read
what they write, don't ask them what they believe, just
observe what they do.

ASHLEY MONTAGU

It is difficult to satisfy one's appetite by painting
pictures of cakes.

Let us develop the resources of our land, call forth its powers,
build up its institutions, promote all its great interests, and see
whether we also, in our day and generation, may not perform
something worthy to be remembered.

DANIEL WEBSTER

That which one most anticipates, soon comes to pass.

The victor feels no fatigue.

Go on deserving applause, and you will be sure to meet
with it; and the way to deserve it is to be good and
to be industrious.

THOMAS JEFFERSON

Nobody can count themselves an artist unless they can carry a
picture in their head before they paint it.

CLAUDE MONET

If you would know the value of money, go and try to borrow
some.

BENJAMIN FRANKLIN

If a man does not know what port he is steering for, no wind is
favorable to him.

SENECA

Never tell people how to do things.
Tell them what to do, and they will surprise you
with their ingenuity.

GENERAL GEORGE PATTON JR.

One today is worth two tomorrows.

BENJAMIN FRANKLIN

Every event that a man would master must be mounted on
the run, and no man ever caught the reins of a thought
except as it galloped past him.

OLIVER WENDELL HOLMES

It takes a lot of energy to say very little.
That's why those who say nothing get so much done.

A fool often fails because he thinks what is difficult is easy,
and a wise man because he thinks what is easy is difficult.

JOHN CHURTON COLLINS

Half the failures in life arise from pulling in one's horse
as he is leaping.

J. C. AND A. W. HARE

From the sublime to the ridiculous is but a step.

NAPOLEON

The road to failure is often decorated by the flowers
of past achievements.

Most failures whom I have known were experts
at making excuses!

Fame is the perfume of heroic deeds.

SOCRATES

We make more progress by owning our faults than
by always dwelling on our virtues.

THOMAS BRACKETT REED

If we are to be a really great people, we must
strive in good faith to play a great part in the world.
We cannot avoid meeting great issues.
All that we can determine for ourselves is whether
we shall meet them well or ill.

THEODORE ROOSEVELT

For every achievement there is a price. For every goal there is
an opponent. For every victory there is a problem. For every
triumph there is sacrifice.

WILLIAM ARTHUR WARD

Better that we should err in action than wholly refuse
to perform. The storm is so much better than the calm, as
it declares the presence of a living principle. Stagnation is
something worse than death. It is corruption also.

WILLIAM GILMORE SIMMS

Whatever you think it's gonna take, double it.
That applies to money, time, stress. It's gonna be harder than
you think and take longer than you think.

RICHARD A. CORTESE

Victories that are cheap are cheap.
Those only are worth having which come as the result
of hard fighting.

HENRY WARD BEECHER

The man who makes no mistakes does not usually make anything. Success has made failures of many men.

CINDY ADAMS

Success is just a matter of luck. Ask any failure.

EARL WILSON

In the space of two days I had evolved two plans, wholly dis-
tinct, both of which were equally feasible. The point I am trying
to bring out is that one does not plan and then try to make circumstances fit those plans. One tries to make plans fit the
circumstances.

GENERAL GEORGE PATTON JR.

There are two doors to opportunity: push and pull.

ADVERSITY

Trouble develops in us the ability to meet it.
It strengthens and matures those it touches.
Trouble frequently finds for us our dearest friends.
We need the night to see the stars.

Adversity and loss make a man wise.

Adversity is the foundation of virtue.

Many can bear adversity, but few contempt.

You cannot avoid what lies in ambush for you.

A common danger produces unity.
The remedy against bad times is to have patience with them.

Jones' Law: The man who smiles when things go wrong has
thought of someone he can blame it on.

The only cure for sorrow is to kill it with patience.

What can't be cured must be endured.

Once we truly know that life is difficult—once we truly understand and accept it—then life is no longer difficult.

M. SCOTT PECK

The fellow who refuses to face a difficulty should not be surprised if it sneaks up and kicks him from behind.

Two in distress make trouble less.

It is by presence of mind in untried emergencies that the
native mettle of a man is tested.

JAMES RUSSELL LOWELL

Every spring has an autumn and every road an ending.

The best eraser in the world is a good night's sleep.

I have told of my failings and mistakes, if only because I have
found that failure is a far better teacher than success.

BERNARD M. BARUCH

Everything is funny as long as it is happening
to somebody else.

WILL ROGERS

Well it has been said that there is no grief like the grief
which does not speak.

HENRY W. LONGFELLOW

To live is to suffer; to survive is to find meaning in suffering.

VIKTOR FRANKEL

Everyone can master a grief but he that has it.

WILLIAM SHAKESPEARE

Grief destroys even a hero.

Like one who takes away a garment on a cold day . . . is one
who sings songs to a heavy heart.

PROVERBS 25:20

Every heart has its own ache.

The best time to stand up to any of life's situations is immediately after you get up from praying on your knees.

When life hands you lemons, make lemonade.

If you find yourself in hot water—take a bath.

Little minds are tamed and subdued by misfortune; but great minds rise above it.

WASHINGTON IRVING

If all our misfortunes were laid in one common heap, whence everyone must take an equal portion, most people would be content to take their own and depart.

SOCRATES

Let us be of good cheer, however, remembering that the misfortunes hardest to bear are those which never come.

JAMES RUSSELL LOWELL

Depend upon it that if a man talks of his misfortunes, there is something in them that is not disagreeable to him.

SAMUEL JOHNSON

Misfortune comes on horseback and goes away on foot.

When misfortune is greatest, relief is nearest.

Mishaps are like knives, that either serve us or cut us, as we grasp them by the blade or the handle.

JAMES RUSSELL LOWELL

When down in the mouth, remember Jonah.
He came out all right.

THOMAS EDISON

A misty morning does not signify a cloudy day.

There is no such thing as a problem that doesn't
have a gift in it.

There's no flood that doesn't recede.

I refuse to believe that problems will solve themselves—I have
never yet solved a problem unless I attacked it head-on.

At the heart of every problem you will find the easiest
answer to its solution.

Most people find that solving problems is no trouble at all—as
long as they are the other fellow's.

It takes both rain and sunshine to make a rainbow.

For every aliment under the sun,
There is a remedy, or there is none;
If there be one, try to find it;
If there be none, never mind it.

DALE CARNEGIE

God, grant me the serenity to accept the things I cannot
change, the courage to change the things I can, and the wisdom to know the difference.

THE SERENITY PRAYER

The world is a great ocean upon which we encounter
more tempestuous storms than calms.

No one would ever have crossed the ocean if he could have
gotten off the ship in the storm.

CHARLES F. KETTERING

I walked a mile with Pleasure—
She chattered all the way
But left me none the wiser
For all she had to say.
I walked a mile with Sorrow
And ne'er a word said she,
But, oh, the things I learned from her
When Sorrow walked with me.

ROBERT BROWNING HAMILTON

The way I see it, if you want the rainbow, you
gotta put up with the rain.

DOLLY PARTON

Life is made up of sobs, sniffles, and smiles, with
sniffles predominating.

O. HENRY

Where there was a storm, there is calm.

A bow long bent grows weak.

It takes the night to bring out the stars.

The only cure for suffering is to face it head on, grasp it
round the neck, and use it.

MARY CRAIG

If you suffer, thank God! It is a sure sign that you are alive.

ELBERT HUBBARD

Into each life some rain must fall.

HENRY W. LONGFELLOW

If pleasures are greatest in anticipation, just remember that
this is also true of trouble.

ELBERT HUBBARD

Troubles are like babies—they grow larger by nursing.

LADY HOLLAND

I have learned much from my teachers, more from my books,
but most from my troubles!

THE MIDRASH

Few days pass without some clouds.

One good day often costs a hundred bad nights.

We cannot direct the wind, but we can adjust our sails.

Moaning over your troubles is silly.
Few persons ever listen to you, and those who do
are apt to like the sound.

What seem to us bitter trials are often blessings in disguise.

OSCAR WILDE

It is said an Eastern monarch once charged his wise men to
invent him a sentence, to be ever in view, and which should be
true and appropriate in all times and situations. They presented
him the words: "And this, too, shall pass away." How much it
expresses! How chastening in the hour of pride—how consoling
in the depth of affliction!

ABRAHAM LINCOLN

Worry is like a rocking chair. It will give you something to do,
but it won't get you anywhere.

Worry does not empty tomorrow of its sorrow; it empties today of its strength.

CORRIE TEN BOOM

Worry, the interest paid by those who borrow trouble.

GEORGE W. LYON

Don't hurry, don't worry. You're only here for a short visit. So be sure to stop and smell the flowers.

WALTER HAGEN

Every evening I turn my worries over to God—because He's going to be up all night anyway.

Most worries are reruns.

How futile is worry? Just try to recall what you were worrying about one year ago today.

Experiencing a great sorrow is like entering a cave. We are overwhelmed by the darkness and the loneliness. We feel that there is no escape from the prison-house of pain. But God in His loving kindness has placed on the invisible wall the lamp of faith, whose beams shall lead us back to the sunlit world, where work and friends and service await us.

HELEN KELLER

ADVICE

Advice is like castor oil,
easy enough to give
but dreadful uneasy to take.

JOSH BILLINGS

Never go to a doctor whose office plants are dead.

ERMA BOMBECK

Never lend your car to anyone to whom you have given birth.

ERMA BOMBECK

When things go wrong, don't go with them.

Begin somewhere; you cannot build a reputation on
what you intend to do.

LIZ SMITH

Quit now, you'll never make it. If you disregard this advice,
you'll be halfway there.

DAVID ZUCKER

Go to bed. What you're staying up for isn't worth it.

ANDY ROONEY

Above all, do not talk yourself out of good ideas by trying to
expound them at haphazard meetings.

JACQUES BARZUN

I always pass on good advice. It is the only thing to do with it.
It is never any use to oneself.

OSCAR WILDE

A good scare is worth more to a man than good advice.

EDGAR WATSON HOWE

The easiest way to escape being hated is to mind your own business and refrain from giving good advice.

W. BURTON BALDRY

Give neither advice nor salt until you are asked for it.

If you want people to notice your faults, start giving advice.

KELLY STEPHENS

How is it possible to expect mankind to take advice when they will not so much as take warning?

JONATHAN SWIFT

We give advice by the bucket, but take it by the grain.

W. R. ALGER

Admonish your friends privately, but praise them openly.

PUBLILIUS SYRUS

Some folks won't ask for advice for fear of giving the impression they need it.

No one wants advice—only corroboration.

JOHN STEINBECK

Both medicine and advice are easy to prescribe but hard to take.

Advice is like snow; the softer it falls, the longer it dwells upon, and the deeper it sinks into the mind.

SAMUEL TAYLOR COLERIDGE

He who builds to every man's advice will have a crooked house.

DANISH PROVERB

For lack of guidance a nation falls, but many advisers make victory sure.

PROVERBS 11:14

One piece of good advice is better than a bag full.

Never trust the advice of a man in difficulties.

AESOP

Whatever your advice, make it brief.

HORACE

Never give advice in a crowd.

ARAB PROVERB

The true secret of giving advice is, after you have honestly given it, to be perfectly indifferent whether it is taken or not.

HANNAH W. SMITH

The advice of the aged will not mislead you.

No one is wise enough to advise himself.

He who works on the highway will have many advisers.

AMERICA

I sought for the greatness and genius of America in her
commodious harbors and her ample rivers—and
it was not there . . . in her fertile fields and boundless forests—
and it was not there . . . in her rich mines and her vast world
commerce—and it was not there . . . in her democratic
Congress and her matchless Constitution—and it was not
there. Not until I went into the churches of America and
heard her pulpits flame with righteousness did I understand
the secret of her genius and power. America is great
because she is good, and if America ever ceases to be good,
America will cease to be great.

ALEXIS DE TOCQUEVILLE

The fabulous country—the place where miracles
not only happen, but where they happen all the time.

THOMAS WOLFE

Whatever America hopes to bring to pass in the world must
first come to pass in the heart of America.

DWIGHT D. EISENHOWER

There is nothing wrong with America that the faith, love of
freedom, intelligence, and energy of her citizens cannot cure.

DWIGHT D. EISENHOWER

God had a divine purpose in placing this land
between two great oceans to be found by those who
had a special love of freedom and courage.

RONALD REAGAN

There is nothing wrong with America
that together we can't fix.

RONALD REAGAN

Americans are getting stronger. Twenty years ago, it took two people to carry ten dollars' worth of groceries. Today, a five-year-old can do it.

HENNY YOUNGMAN

The winds that blow through the wide sky in these mountains— the winds that sweep from Canada to Mexico, from the Pacific to the Atlantic—have always blown on free men.

FRANKLIN D. ROOSEVELT

America is the only country ever founded on the printed word.

MARSHALL MCLUHAN

America is the great melting pot.

ISRAEL ZANQUILL

I believe in America because we have great dreams—and because we have the opportunity to make those dreams come true.

WENDELL L. WILLKIE

Then conquer we must, for our cause is just, and this be our motto: "In God is our trust!"

FRANCIS SCOTT KEY

If we do not make a common cause to save the good old ship of the Union on this voyage, nobody will have a chance to pilot her on another voyage.

ABRAHAM LINCOLN

And so, my fellow Americans: Ask not what your country can do for you—ask what you can do for your country. My fellow citizens of the world: Ask not what America will do for you, but what together we can do for the freedom of man.

JOHN F. KENNEDY

The only foes that threaten America are the enemies at home, and these are ignorance, superstition and incompetence.

ELBERT HUBBARD

The second day of July, 1776, will be the most memorable epoch in the history of America. I am apt to believe that it will be celebrated by succeeding generations as the great anniversary festival. It ought to be commemorated as the day of deliverance, by solemn acts of devotion to God Almighty.

It ought to be solemnized with pomp and parade, with shows, games, sports, guns, bells, bonfires, and illustrations, from one end of this continent to the other, from this time forward forevermore.

JOHN ADAMS

America is the only country in the world where a man can afford to build a four-bedroom house by the time all of his children are old enough to go to college.

Americanism means the virtues of courage, honor, justice, truth, sincerity, and hardihood—the virtues that made America. The things that will destroy America are prosperity-at-any-price, peace-at-any-price, safety-first instead of duty-first, the love of soft living and the get-rich-quick theory of life.

THEODORE ROOSEVELT

There can be no fifty-fifty Americanism in this country. There is room here for only 100 percent Americanism, only for those who are Americans and nothing else.

THEODORE ROOSEVELT

I venture to suggest that patriotism is not a short and frenzied outburst of emotion but the tranquil and steady dedication of a lifetime.

ADLAI STEVENSON

Patriotism depends as much on mutual suffering as on mutual success, and it is by that experience of all fortunes and all feelings that a great national character is created.

BENJAMIN DISRAELI

Patriotism consists not in waving the flag, but in striving that our country shall be righteous as well as strong.

JAMES BRYCE

Patriotism is a mighty precious thing when it costs nothing, but the mass of mankind consider it a very foolish thing when it curtails their self-indulgence.

JOHN BROKENBROUGH

The patriots are those who love America enough to wish to see her as a model to mankind.

ADLAI STEVENSON

It having pleased the Almighty ruler of the Universe propitiously to defend the cause of the United American States and finally by raising us up a powerful friend among the princes of the earth to establish our liberty and independence upon lasting foundations, it becomes us to set apart a day for gratefully acknowledging the divine goodness and celebrating the important event which we owe to His benign Interposition.

Any well-established village in New England or the Northern Middle West could afford a town drunkard, a town atheist, and a few Democrats.

DENIS WILLIAM BROGAN

You may be Southern—but you're no comfort.

DICK GREGORY

The United States never lost a war or won a conference.

WILL ROGERS

[An Englishman is] a person who does things because they have been done before. [An American is] a person who does things because they haven't been done before.

MARK TWAIN

My God! How little do my countrymen know what precious blessings they are in possession of, and which no other people on earth enjoy. I confess I had no idea of it myself. While we shall see multiplied instances of Europeans going to live in America, I will venture to say no man now living will ever see an instance of an American removing to settle in Europe and continuing there.

THOMAS JEFFERSON

We have been the recipients of the choicest bounties of Heaven. We have been preserved, these many years, in peace and prosperity. We have grown in numbers, wealth and power, as no other nation has ever grown. But we have forgotten God. We have forgotten the gracious hand which preserved us in peace, and multiplied and enriched and strengthened us; and we have vainly imagined, in the deceitfulness of our hearts, that all these blessings were produced by some superior wisdom and virtue of our own. Intoxicated with unbroken success, we have become too self-sufficient to feel the necessity of redeeming and preserving grace, too proud to pray to the God that made us!

ABRAHAM LINCOLN

Let us have done with British-Americans and Irish-Americans and German-Americans, and so on, and all be Americans . . . If a man is going to be an American at all let him be so without any qualifying adjectives; and if he is going to be something else, let him drop the word American from his personal description.

HENRY CABOT LODGE

Not many Americans have been around the world but their money sure has.

WALTER SLEZAK

If the American people ever allow private banks to control the issuance of their currency, first by inflation and then by deflation, the banks and corporations that will grow up around them will deprive the people of all their property until their children will wake up homeless on the continent their fathers conquered.

THOMAS JEFFERSON

If I were to attempt to put my political philosophy tonight into a single phrase, it would be this: Trust the people. Trust their good sense, their decency, their fortitude, their faith. Trust them with the facts. Trust them with the great decisions. And fix as our guiding star the passion to create a society where people can fulfill their own best selves—where no American is held down by race or color, by worldly condition or social status, from gaining what his character earns him as an American citizen, as a human being and as a child of God.

ADLAI STEVENSON

When at first you don't succeed, remember the last four letters of American.

The United States is the only country with a known birthday.

JAMES G. BLAINE

After what I owe to God, nothing should be more dear or more sacred to me than the love and respect I owe my country.

JACQUES AUGUSTE DE THOU

Double—no triple—our troubles and we'd still be better off than any other people on earth.

With malice toward none, with charity for all, with firmness in the right—as God gives us to see the right—let us strive on to finish the work we are in, to bind up the nation's wounds, to care for him who shall have borne the battle and for his widow and his orphan—to do all which may achieve and cherish a just and lasting peace among ourselves and with all nations.

ABRAHAM LINCOLN

Peace is a blessing, and like most blessings, it must be earned.

DWIGHT D. EISENHOWER

Peace, above all things, is to be desired, but blood must sometimes be spilled to obtain it on equable and lasting terms.

ANDREW JACKSON

Professional pacifists, the peace-at-any-price, nonresistance, universal arbitration people, are seeking to Chinafy this country.

THEODORE ROOSEVELT

If we desire to avoid insult, we must be able to repel it; if we desire to secure peace, one of the most powerful instruments of our rising prosperity, it must be known that we are at all times ready for war.

GEORGE WASHINGTON

ATTITUDE

Every forward step achieved by man
has been due to the adventurous attitude.
This attitude inspires dissatisfaction
with the world as it is; it arouses the
desire to change and improve things.
The attitude of adventure is the flame
that lights the fuse to explode new ideas.

WILFRED A. PETERSON

Keep your face to the sunshine, and
you cannot see the shadow.

HELEN KELLER

If your capacity to acquire has outstripped your capacity to
enjoy, you are on the way to the scrap heap.

GLENN BUCK

The winners in life think constantly in terms of
"I can," "I will," and "I am."
Losers, on the other hand, concentrate their waking thoughts
on what they should have done or what they don't do.

DENIS WAITLEY

Few people succeed in business unless they enjoy their work.

A chip on the shoulder is the heaviest load a man can carry.

There are two ways of meeting difficulties.
You alter the difficulties, or you alter yourself to meet them.

PHYLISS BOTTOME

Nothing controls another person's mood like the expression
on your own face.

If life were predictable, it would cease to be life and
would be without flavor.

ELEANOR ROOSEVELT

Life is 10 percent what you make it and
90 percent how you take it.

The mind grows by what it feeds on.

JOSIAH GILBERT HOLLAND

Life is a disease, and the only difference between one man and
another is the stage of the disease at which he lives.

GEORGE BERNARD SHAW

The optimist pleasantly ponders how high his kite will fly; the
pessimist woefully wonders how soon his kite will fall.

WILLIAM ARTHUR WARD

An optimist is one who gets tread by a lion but
enjoys the scenery.

What a man thinks of himself, that it is which
determines, or rather indicates, his fate.

HENRY DAVID THOREAU

He who is in the shade doesn't know
that another is in the sun.

Today is the first day of the rest of your life.

Agree, for the law is costly.

Acceptance of what has happened is the first step to overcoming the consequences of any misfortune.

WILLIAM JAMES

Better a lean agreement than a fat lawsuit.

Better to eat bread in peace than cake amidst turmoil.

When I grow up, I want to be a little boy.

A man is not defeated by his opponents but by himself.

As a general rule, I abstain from reading the reports of attacks upon myself, wishing not to be provoked by that to which I cannot properly offer an answer.

The world is full of cactus, but we don't have to sit on it.

WILL FOLEY

All of the days of the oppressed are wretched, but the cheerful heart has a continual feast.

PROVERBS 15:15

All you need is to tell a man that he is no good ten times a day, and very soon he begins to believe it himself.

LIN YUTANG

Like an earring of gold or an ornament of fine gold is a wise man's rebuke to a listening ear.

PROVERBS 25:12

The real enjoyment of living, like the real enjoyment of eating a steak, comes when you put your teeth into it.

When Abraham Lincoln was a candidate for President of the United States, someone asked him about his aspiration to that high office. He answered that he did not fear his opponents. "But," he said, "there is a man named Lincoln of whom I am very much afraid. If I am defeated, it will be by that man."

DILLARD S. MILLER

Only those are fit to live who do not fear to die; and none are fit to die who have shrunk from the joy of life and the duty of life. Both life and death are parts of the same Great Adventure.

THEODORE ROOSEVELT

CAUTION

Wherever there is danger, there
lurks opportunity; whenever there
is opportunity, there lurks danger.
The two are inseparable; they go together.

EARL NIGHTINGALE

Can a man scoop fire into his lap without
his clothes being burned? Can a man walk on hot coals
without his feet being scorched?
So is he who sleeps with another man's wife.

PROVERBS 6:27-29

Before undergoing a surgical operation, arrange your temporal
affairs. You may live.

AMBROSE BIERCE

Those who pry into other people's affairs will hear
what they do not like.

The man who eavesdrops hears himself discussed.

Appetite comes with eating.

He that makes himself an ass must not take it ill
if men ride him.

THOMAS FULLER

Necessity never made a good bargain.

BENJAMIN FRANKLIN

The belly overrules the head.

Temptations are like bargains. You never know how badly you're being stung until after you've fallen for them.

The man who says what he thinks is finished, and the man who thinks what he says is an idiot.

ROLF HOCHHUTH

When the cat has gone, the rats come out to stretch themselves.

The only difference between a rut and a grave is their dimensions.

ELLEN GLASGOW

Who often changes, damages.

Never contend with a man who has nothing to lose.

GRACIAN

He who puts up security for another will surely suffer, but whoever refuses to strike hands in pledge is safe.

PROVERBS 11:15

Do not be a man who strikes hands in pledge or puts up security for debts; if you lack the means to pay, your very bed will be snatched from under you.

PROVERBS 22:26-27

When the danger past, God is forgotten.

DANIEL WEBSTER

Better to break off an engagement than a marriage.

Of two evils, choose neither.

CHARLES H. SPURGEON

Beware of little expenses; a small leak will sink a great ship.

BENJAMIN FRANKLIN

Don't make yourself a mouse or the cat will eat you.

A halo has to fall only a few inches to become a noose.

FARMERS' ALMANAC

Opportunity is a hit-or-miss proposition; whereas
temptation likes to linger around indefinitely.

There is a paradox in pride: It makes some men ridiculous
but prevents others from becoming so.

C. C. COLTON

"I did that," says my memory. "I could not have done that,"
says my pride, and remains inexorable.
Eventually—the memory yields.

FRIEDRICH W. NIETZSCHE

Pride is at the bottom of all great mistakes.

JOHN RUSKIN

The prouder a man is, the more he thinks he deserves; and the
more he thinks he deserves, the less he really does deserve.

HENRY WARD BEECHER

You can always tell a proud man—but you can't
tell him much!

There is but a step between a proud man's glory
and his disgrace.

PUBLILIUS SYRUS

Beware of the danger signals that flag problems: silence, secretiveness, or sudden outburst.

SYLVIA PORTER

Too late repents the rat when caught by the cat.

JOHN FLORIO

For of all sad words of tongue or pen, the saddest are these: "It might have been."

JOHN GREENLEAF WHITTIER

A thousand regrets do not pay one debt.

From trivial things great contests oft arise.

If there's bitterness in the heart, sugar in the mouth won't make life sweeter.

Every man has his price. This is not true. But for every man there exists a bait which he cannot resist swallowing.

FRIEDRICH W. NIETZSCHE

Give me six lines written by the most honorable of men, and I will find an excuse in them to hang him.

CARDINAL RICHELIEU

The best way to keep on the sunny side of life is to walk away from shady deals.

Lust is bottomless.

Money lays waste cities; it sets men to roaming from home; it seduces and corrupts honest men and turns virtue to baseness; it teaches villainy and impiety.

SOPHOCLES

The love of money is a root of all kinds of evil.

1 TIMOTHY 6:10

There are persons who constantly clamor. They complain of oppression, speculation, and pernicious influence of wealth. They cry out loudly against all banks and corporations, and a means by which small capitalists become united in order to produce important and beneficial results. They carry on mad hostility against all established institutions. They would choke the fountain of human civilization.

The time to guard against corruption and tyranny is before they have gotten hold of us. It is better to keep the wolf out of the fold than to trust to drawing his teeth and talons after he shall have entered.

THOMAS JEFFERSON

Wounded vanity knows when it is mortally hurt and limps off the field, piteous, all disguises thrown away. But pride carries its banner to the last, and, fast as it is driven from one field, unfurls it in another.

HELEN HUNT JACKSON

CHARACTER

Character is like a tree, and
reputation is like a shadow. The
shadow is what we think of it;
the tree is the real thing.

ABRAHAM LINCOLN

To blame is easy; to do it better is difficult.

If you would not be forgotten as soon as you are dead, either
write things worth reading or do things worth writing.

BENJAMIN FRANKLIN

A man lays the foundation of true greatness when
he becomes more concerned with building his character
than with expanding his reputation.

WILLIAM ARTHUR WARD

You can't tell what a man is like or what he is thinking
when you are looking at him. You must get around behind him
and see what he has been looking at.

WILL ROGERS

Ugliness with a good character is better than beauty.

MARION DE VELDER

Character is long-standing habit.

PLUTARCH

Every man is a volume, if you know how to read him.

WILLIAM ELLERY CHANNING

Education commences at the mother's knee, and
every word spoken within the hearing of little children tends
towards the formation of character.

HOSEA BALLOU

Resolved never to do anything which I should be afraid to do
if it were the last hour of my life.

JONATHAN EDWARDS

Some men are born mediocre, some men achieve mediocrity,
and some men have mediocrity thrust upon them.

JOSEPH HELLER

We can tell our values by looking at our checkbook stubs.

GLORIA STEINEM

I cannot believe that the purpose of life is to be "happy."
I think the purpose of life is to be useful, to be responsible, to
be honorable, to be compassionate.
It is, after all, to matter: to count, to stand for something, to
have made some difference that you lived at all.

LEO C. ROSTEN

A man never discloses his own character so clearly as when he
describes another's.

JEAN PAUL RICHTER

Underneath this flabby exterior is an
enormous lack of character.

OSCAR LEVANT

Character is made by what you stand for; reputation, by
what you fall for.

ROBERT QUILLEN

Character is what you are in the dark.

DWIGHT L. MOODY

Never add the weight of your character to a charge against a
person without knowing it to be true.

ABRAHAM LINCOLN

These are times in which a genius would wish to live.
It is not in the still calm of life, or
the repose of a pacific station, that
great characters are formed . . .
Great necessities call our great virtues.

ABIGAIL ADAMS

Character contributes to beauty.
It fortifies a woman as her youth fades.
A mode of conduct, a standard of courage, discipline,
fortitude, and integrity can do a great deal
to make a woman beautiful.

JACQUELINE BISSET

Gross and obscure natures, however decorated, seem impure
shambles; but character gives splendor to youth and awe to
wrinkled skin and gray hairs.

RALPH WALDO EMERSON

I have a dream that my four little children will
one day live in a nation where they will not be judged by the
color of their skin, but by the content of their character.

MARTIN LUTHER KING JR.

There is no odor so bad as that which arises
from goodness tainted.

HENRY DAVID THOREAU

CHARACTER

How a man plays the game shows something of his character;
how he loses shows all of it.

GEORGIA TRIBUNE

Character is the ability to win an argument by
keeping your mouth shut.

A good character is more valuable than gold.

There is so much good in the worst of us,
And so much bad in the best of us,
That it ill behooves any of us
To find fault with the rest of us.

We attract hearts to the qualities we display; we retain them
by the qualities we possess.

SCAD

He that lives well, is learned enough.

BENJAMIN FRANKLIN

Give to us clear vision that we may know where to stand and
what to stand for—because unless we stand for something, we
shall fall for anything.

PETER MARSHALL

I have simply tried to do what seemed best each day, as
each day came.

ABRAHAM LINCOLN

Tell me what you are eager to buy, and I will tell you
what you are.

A good example is the best sermon.

BENJAMIN FRANKLIN

The less justified a man is in claiming excellence for his own self, the more ready is he to claim all excellence for his nation, his religion, his race, or his holy cause.

ERIC HOFFER

Do you see a man wise in his own eyes?
There is more hope for a fool than for him.

PROVERBS 26:12

Decency, generosity, cooperation, assistance in trouble, devotion to duty—these are the things that are of greater value than surface appearances and customs.

DWIGHT D. EISENHOWER

Whenever you are to do a thing, though it can never be known but to yourself, ask yourself how you would act were all the world looking at you and act accordingly.

THOMAS JEFFERSON

Sow a thought, you reap an act; sow an act, you reap a habit; sow a habit, you reap a character; sow a character, you reap a destiny.

What a man has been is history; what he does is law; what he is is philosophy; what he ought to be is ethics.

EUGENE P. BERTIN

Few things are harder to put up with than the annoyance of a good example.

MARK TWAIN

We can't all be shining examples, but we can at least twinkle a little.

People are stimulated by example—those under you won't
work unless you do.

The expression a woman wears on her face is far more
important than the clothes she wears on her back.

DALE CARNEGIE

There is never an instant's truce between virtue and vice.
Goodness is the only investment that never fails.

HENRY DAVID THOREAU

The reputation of a thousand years may be determined by the
conduct of one hour.

JAPANESE PROVERB

Associate with men of good quality, if
you esteem your own reputation, for it is better to
be alone than in bad company.

GEORGE WASHINGTON

Glass, china, and reputation are easily crack'd and
never well mended.

BENJAMIN FRANKLIN

Never speak ill of yourself; your friends will always say
enough on that subject.

CHARLES MAURICE DE TALLEYRAND

A good name is more desirable than great riches; to
be esteemed is better than silver or gold.

PROVERBS 22:1

Any man will command respect if he takes a stand and
backs it up with his life.

BOBBY RICHARDSON

Where we do not respect, we cease to love.

BENJAMIN DISRAELI

It is a grand mistake to think of being great without goodness, and I pronounce it as certain that there was never yet a truly great man that was not at the same time truly virtuous.

BENJAMIN FRANKLIN

Everything I say, you know, goes into print. If I make a mistake it doesn't merely affect me or you, but the country. I therefore ought at least try not to make mistakes.

ABRAHAM LINCOLN

I'd rather see a sermon than hear one any day;
I'd rather one should walk with me than merely show the way.
The eye's a better pupil and more willing than the ear;
Fine counsel is confusing, but example's always clear.
And the best of all preachers are the men who live their
  creeds,
For to see the good in action is what everybody needs.
I can soon learn how to do it if you'll let me see it done;
I can watch your hands in action, but your tongue too fast
  may run.
And the lectures you deliver may be very wise and true,
But I'd rather get my lesson by observing what you do.
For I may misunderstand you and the high advice you give,
But there's no misunderstanding how you act and how you
  live.

THE LOOKOUT

Every tub must stand on its own bottom.

Try not to become a man of success but rather
try to become a man of value.

ALBERT EINSTEIN

Cultivate in yourself the qualities you admire most in others.

ARNOLD GLASON

It's a long way from words to deeds.

Plant patience in the garden of thy soul!
The roots are bitter, but the fruit is sweet!
And when at last it stands a tree complete,
Beneath its tender shade the burning heat
And burden of the day shall lose control—
Plant patience in the garden of thy soul!

HENRY AUSTIN

The longest day must have an end.

He that can have patience, can have what he will.

BENJAMIN FRANKLIN

There are two kinds of people in one's life: people
whom one keeps waiting and the people for whom one waits.

S. N. BEHRMAN

Beware the fury of a patient man.

JOHN DRYDEN

A patient person is one who is willing to let somebody teach
him something he already knows.

If all the gold in the world were melted down into a solid cube
it would be about the size of an eight-room house. If a man got
possession of all that gold—billions of dollars' worth—he could
not buy a friend, character, peace of mind, clear conscience, or
a sense of eternity.

CHARLES F. BANNING

I had laid it down as a law to myself, to take no notice of the thousand calumnies issued against me, but to trust my character to my own conduct, and the good sense and candor of my fellow citizens.

THOMAS JEFFERSON

There is no character, howsoever good and fine, but it can be destroyed by ridicule, howsoever poor and witless. Observe the ass, for instance: His character is about perfect; he is the choicest spirit among all the humbler animals; yet see what ridicule has brought him to. Instead of feeling complimented when we are called an ass, we are left in doubt.

MARK TWAIN

Good character is more to be praised than outstanding talent. Most talents are to some extent a gift. Good character, by contrast, is not given to us. We have to build it piece by piece . . . by thought, choice, courage, and determination.

JOHN LUTHER

Discouragements and obstacles can be used to strengthen character as dams make it possible for rivers to generate electricity: They impede the flow but they increase the power. Defeats are inescapable; failures are as certain as the sparks fly upward. By the side of every mountain is a valley, and by the side of every oasis is a desert.

COMMON SENSE

Men are made stronger on realization
that the helping hand they need is
at the end of their own right arm.

SIDNEY PHILLIPS

Better lose the anchor than the whole ship.

To assume is to be deceived.

On a good bargain, think twice.

Beauty, in a modest woman, is like fire, or a sharp sword at a
distance: neither doth the one burn, nor the other wound
those that come not too near them.

MIGUEL DE CERVANTES

As you make your bed, so you must lie on it.

So live that you wouldn't be ashamed to sell the family parrot
to the town gossip.

WILL ROGERS

The illusion that the times that were are better than those
that are, has probably pervaded all ages.

HORACE GREELEY

A bird in the nest is better than one hundred flying.

The empty cask makes the most sound.

JACOB CATS

Believe a boaster as you would a liar.

He will soon be a beggar that cannot say no.

Where is human nature so weak as in the bookstore!

HENRY WARD BEECHER

Idealism increases in direct proportion to one's
distance from the problem.

Perhaps the world's second worst crime is boredom.
The first is being a bore.

CECIL BEATON

Who readily borrows, readily lies.

Borrowing is a wedding; paying back is mourning.

He who is quick at borrowing, is slow in paying.

Of course all boys are not full of tricks, but
the best of them are. That is, those who are readiest to
play innocent jokes, and who are continually looking
for chances to make Rome howl, are the most apt
to be first-class businessmen.

GEORGE W. PECK

The human brain starts working the moment you are born and
never stops until you stand up to speak in public.

SIR GEORGE JESSEL

If humble pie has to be eaten, that's the best way to eat it—
bolt it whole.

MAURICE HEWLETT

Nobody on his deathbed has said, "I wish I had spent
more time with my business."

People always are motivated by at least two things: the
one they tell you about, and
the one they don't tell you about.

Everyone lays a burden on the willing horse.

Every time I run across a man with a chip on his shoulder I
look for wood higher up.

Who buys cheap pays twice.

The buyer needs a hundred eyes, the seller but one.

One can get sick of cake but never of bread.

He that will cheat at play, will cheat you any way.

Cleaning your house while your kids are still growing is like
shoveling the walk before it stops snowing.

PHYLLIS DILLER

I always did think that cleverness was the art of
hiding ignorance.

SHELLAND BRADLEY

It is very clever to know how to hide one's cleverness.

LA ROCHEFOUCAULD

It is poor comfort for one who has broken his leg that
another has broken his neck.

Common sense is compelled to make its way without the
enthusiasm of anyone; all admit it grudgingly.

EDGAR WATSON HOWE

Talk low, talk slow, and don't say too much.

JOHN WAYNE

Of all human powers operating on the affairs of mankind,
none is greater than that of competition.

HENRY CLAY

Conceit is God's gift to little men.

BRUCE BARTON

The fellow who jumps to conclusions is not always certain
of a happy landing.

Contentment is an inexhaustible treasure.

The best contraceptive is the word no—repeated frequently.

MARGARET SMITH

Look out fer th' feller who lets you do all th' talkin'.

FRANK MCKINNEY

Correction is good when administered in time.

The way of the criminal is hard, but then, so is
any other well-beaten path.

It is the height of absurdity to sow little but weeds in
the first half of one's lifetime and expect to harvest
a valuable crop in the second half.

PERCY H. JOHNSTON

A chip on the shoulder is too heavy a
piece of baggage to carry through life.

B. C. FORBES

He who would not go to hell, must not go to court.

If the devil catch a man idle, he'll set him at work.

Half a fool is worse than a whole one.

He who would make a fool of himself will find many to help him.

Foolishness grows by itself; no need to sow it.

If a fool has a hump nobody notices it; if the wise man has a pimple everybody talks about it.

To lengthen thy life, lessen thy meals.

BENJAMIN FRANKLIN

A man too busy to take care of his health is like a mechanic too busy to take care of his tools.

SPANISH PROVERB

He that inquires much, learns much.

Nobody works as hard for his money as the man who marries it.

FRANK MCKINNEY HUBBARD

Most of us know how to say nothing; few of us know when.

My head keeps making dates that my body can't keep.

Let another praise you, and not your own mouth; someone else, and not your own lips.

PROVERBS 27:2

What gets rewarded, gets done.

He who knows the road can ride full trot.

Time flies; but remember, you are the navigator.

The dogs bark, but the caravan goes on.

INDIAN PROVERB

A critic is a legless man who teaches running.

CHANNING POLLOCK

People are in great danger when they know what
they should do and refuse to act upon what they know.

JAMES BALDWIN

Death is nature's way of telling you to slow down.

GRAFFITO

Six feet of earth make all men equal.

He that dies pays all debts.

WILLIAM SHAKESPEARE

People who think nothing of going into debt are
usually even less concerned about getting out of it.

Nothing makes some people go into debt like trying to keep
up with people who already are.

Always borrow from a pessimist—he never expects it back.

Experience teaches us that the man who looks you
straight in the eye, particularly if he adds a
firm handshake, is hiding something.

CLIFTON FADIMAN

If a man deceive me once, shame on him; but if
he deceive me twice, shame on me.

When a person tells you, 'I'll think it over and let you
know'— you know.

OLIN MILLER

If you see a snake, just kill it—don't appoint
a committee on snakes.

H. ROSS PEROT

Diets are for those who are thick and tired of it.

Let everyone sweep in front of his own door, and
the world will be clean.

Noble deeds and hot baths are the best cures for depression.

DODIE SMITH

Better keep the devil at the door than
turn him out of the house.

He that is embarked with the devil must sail with him.

A man's worst difficulties begin when he is able
to do as he likes.

T. H. HUXLEY

If you want your dinner, don't offend the cook.

Most of us would rather risk catastrophe than
read the directions.

Throw dirt enough and some will stick.

Every donkey loves to hear himself bray.

He that lies down with dogs will get up with fleas.

The fellow who growls all day long is bound to be
dog-tired by the end of the day.

Make yourself a donkey, and everyone will
lay his sack on you.

Saving is a very fine thing.
Especially when your parents have done it for you.

WINSTON CHURCHILL

Nothing will make a man put his best foot forward
like getting the other one in hot water.

Put all your eggs in one basket, and—watch the basket.

MARK TWAIN

He that will have eggs, must bear with cackling.

Why can't we build orphanages next to homes for the elderly?
If someone's sitting in a rocker, it won't be long
before a kid will be in his lap.

CLORIS LEACHMAN

Your enemy makes you wise.

Solitude is a reward you can enjoy just by being punctual.

Several excuses are always less convincing than one.

ALDOUS HUXLEY

Make three correct guesses consecutively, and
you will establish a reputation as an expert.

LAURENCE J. PETER

A stranger's eye sees clearest.

Men are born with two eyes, but with one tongue, in order that they should see twice as much as they say.

The eye of the thief glances about.

He who answers before listening—that is his folly and his shame.

PROVERBS 18:13

The first to present his case seems right, till another comes forward and questions him.

PROVERBS 18:17

Faults are thick where love is thin.

DANISH PROVERB

The greatest of faults is to be conscious of none.

THOMAS CARLYLE

He that dances must pay the fiddler.

If you do not gather firewood, you cannot keep warm.

A fish is caught by its mouth, a man by his words.

The best way in which to silence any friend of yours whom you know to be a fool is to induce him to hire a hall. Nothing chills pretense like exposure.

WOODROW WILSON

A fox should not be on the jury at a goose's trial.

If you would catch a fox you must hunt with geese.

There are two times in a man's life when he should not
speculate: when he can't afford it, and when he can.

MARK TWAIN

A man is in general better pleased when he has a good dinner
upon his table than when his wife speaks Greek.

SAMUEL JOHNSON

A cheerful heart is a good medicine, but a downcast spirit
dries up the bones.

PROVERBS 17:22

Lots of people know a good thing the minute the
other fellow sees it first.

JOB E. HEDGES

Some people will believe anything if you whisper it to them.

LOUIS B. NIZER

Absolute knowledge have I none.
But my aunt's washerwoman's sister's son
Heard a policeman on his beat
Say to a laborer on the street
That he had a letter just last week—
A letter that he did not seek—
From a Chinese merchant in Timbuktu,
Who said that his brother in Cuba knew
Of an Indian chief in a Texan town,
Who got the dope from a circus clown,
That a man in Klondike had it straight
From a guy in a South American state,
That a wild man over in Borneo
Was told by a woman who claimed to know
. . . etc., etc.

Hating people is like burning down your own house
to get rid of a rat.

HARRY EMERSON FOSDICK

Honor is a badge that you cannot pin on yourself.

Meeting expenses is easy—it's avoiding them that's difficult.

Information's pretty thin stuff, unless mixed with experience.

CLARENCE DAY

Prosperity is the surest breeder of insolence I know.

MARK TWAIN

Like one who seizes a dog by the ears is a passer-by who
meddles in a quarrel not his own.

PROVERBS 26:17

The sound of a kiss is not so loud as that of a cannon, but its
echo lasts longer.

OLIVER WENDELL HOLMES

The law turns on golden wheels.

Everyone is wiser after the lawsuit is ended.

Sin has many tools, but a lie is the handle which fits them all.

OLIVER WENDELL HOLMES

The principal difference between a cat and a lie is
that a cat has only nine lives.

MARK TWAIN

Some people go through life standing
at the complaint counter.

Gold goes in at any gate except heaven's.

Everybody claims they're being logical, especially when they're in complete disagreement with you.

Don't go around with a chip on your shoulder; people might think it came off your head.

CHANGING TIMES

If you will stir up the mire, you must bear the smell.

A man does not look behind the door unless he has stood there himself.

I have found that it is not entirely safe, when one is misrepresented under his very nose, to allow the misrepresentation to go uncontradicted.

ABRAHAM LINCOLN

Drive out the mocker, and out goes strife; quarrels and insults are ended.

PROVERBS 22:10

Modesty is the only sure bait when you angle for praise.

LORD CHESTERFIELD

What money can and cannot buy:
A bed but not sleep,
Books but not brains,
Food but not appetite,
Finery but not beauty,
A house but not a home,
Medicine but not health,
Luxuries but not culture,
Amusements but not happiness,
Boon companions but not friends,
Flattery but not respect.

When a fellow says it ain't the money but the principle o' the thing, it's th' money.

KIN HUBBARD

Strange that we call money "dough."
Dough sticks to your fingers.

If you keep your mouth shut, you will never put your foot in it.

AUSTIN O'MALLEY

Who has no money in his purse must have honey in his mouth.

A good name comes after a while, but a
bad name is soon obtained.

When a man tells me he's going to put all his cards on the table, I always look up his sleeve.

LORD HORE-BELISHA

Love your neighbor, yet don't pull down your hedge.

BENJAMIN FRANKLIN

No matter how thin you slice it, it's still baloney.

ALFRED E. SMITH

It's a good thing to have an open mind—but
not so open that your brains fall out.

NEILSON

Opinions are like noses—everyone has one.

Burn a candle at both ends, and it will not last long.

Pinch yourself and know how others feel.

JAPANESE PROVERB

In many ways, mastering paradox is nothing more than having good common sense.

DONALD T. PHILLIPS

Better to have an ugly patch than a beautiful hole.

If you pay in peanuts you must expect to get a monkey.

LESLIE COULTHARD

One pig knows another.

He who digs a pit for others falls into it himself.

I don't think you can spend yourself rich.

GEORGE HUMPHREY

He that goes barefoot must not plant thorns.

GEORGE HERBERT

When you have got an elephant by the hind leg, and he is trying to run away, it's best to let him run.

ABRAHAM LINCOLN

The quarrel that doesn't concern you is pleasant to hear about.

He who asks a question is a fool for five minutes; he who does not ask a question remains a fool forever.

CHINESE PROVERB

Avoid a questioner, for such a man is also a tattler.

HORACE

Every question requires not an answer.

A new broom sweeps clean.

Anyone who says he isn't going to resign,
four times, definitely will.

JOHN KENNETH GALBRAITH

In a calm sea every man is a pilot.

That man is the richest whose pleasures are the cheapest.

HENRY DAVID THOREAU

He who builds by the roadside has many surveyors.

Talk like Robin Hood when you can shoot his bow.

He who sits among the rubbish must not be surprised
if pigs devour him.

Too many sailors drive the boat up the mountain.

He who says what he likes shall hear what he does not like.

We all like to see people seasick when we are not ourselves.

MARK TWAIN

He that seeks, finds, and sometimes what he would rather not.

Seeing ourselves as others see us is usually a terrible letdown.

Until the donkey tried to clear
The fence, he thought himself a deer.

ARTHUR GUITERMAN

He that serves well need not be afraid to ask his wages.

If the shoe fits, wear it.
Where there was a skunk there is a smell.

Beware of a man who does not talk and of a dog
that does not bark.

JACOB CATS

Silence is not always golden. Sometimes it means simply that
the other fellow didn't listen to a word you said.

You can be sincere and still be stupid.

CHARLES KETTERING

Elephants are always drawn smaller than life, but
a flea always larger.

JONATHAN SWIFT

He who slings mud generally loses ground.

ADLAI STEVENSON

One may smile, and smile, and be a villain.

WILLIAM SHAKESPEARE

As you sow, so will you reap.

Two great talkers will not travel far together.

GEORGE BORROW

Many a man's tongue broke his nose.

SEUMAS MACMANUS

He who speaks ill of himself is praised by no one.

The wheel that squeaks the loudest
Is the one that gets the grease.

HENRY WHEELER SHAW

To carry a worry to bed is to sleep with a pack on your back.
Sleep is the best doctor.

Temptations are sure to ring your doorbell, but
it is your fault if you invite them in for dinner.

MEGIDDO MESSAGE

If you desire many things, many things will seem but a few.

BENJAMIN FRANKLIN

He who rides the tiger finds it difficult to dismount.

The reason the way of the transgressor is
so hard is the traffic on it is so heavy.

What I truly value, I do.

You observe a lot by watching.

LAWRENCE P. "YOGI" BERRA

The most effective water power in the world—women's tears.

WILSON MIZNER

Every man can rule an ill wife but him that has her.

JOHN RAY

If wishes were horses, beggars would ride.

Who keeps company with the wolf will learn to howl.

The wrongdoer never lacks excuses.

A growing youth has a wolf in his belly.

Everyone likes a compliment.

ABRAHAM LINCOLN

The secret of patience: to do something else in the meantime.

There are several good protections against temptation, but
the surest is cowardice.

MARK TWAIN

To escape criticism—do nothing, say nothing, be nothing.

ELBERT HUBBARD

Any jackass can kick down a barn, but it
takes a good carpenter to build one.

SAM RAYBURN

Speak little, do much.

BENJAMIN FRANKLIN

Diplomacy: the art of saying "Nice doggie" till
you can find a rock.

WYNN CATLIN

Nothing makes a person respond more creatively than a level
of discontent that approaches the unbearable.

Blessed is he who expects no gratitude, for
he shall not be disappointed.

W. C. BENNETT

A smart girl is one who can hold a man at arm's length
without losing her grip on him.

Put your hand quickly to your hat and slowly to your purse.

DANISH PROVERB

You know that a man has a block of wood on his shoulders
when you hear him whittling down others.
He that has a head of butter must not come near the oven.

Children have never been very good at listening to their elders, but they have never failed to imitate them.

JAMES BALDWIN

Many persons who are good at arithmetic do not know how to count even ten of their blessings.

Remember the end never really justifies the meanness.

He who sows little, reaps little.

They say I tell a great many stories. I reckon I do; but I have learned from long experience that plain people, take them as they run, are more easily influenced through the medium of a broad and humorous illustration than in any other way.

ABRAHAM LINCOLN

COURAGE

I love the man that can smile in trouble,
that can gather strength from distress,
and grow brave by reflection. 'Tis the
business of little minds to shrink; but
he whose heart is firm, and whose
conscience approves his conduct, will
pursue his principles unto death.

THOMAS PAINE

My life is like a stroll upon the beach,
As near the ocean's edge as I can go.

HENRY DAVID THOREAU

A bashful cat makes a proud mouse.

Half the misery in the world comes of want of courage to
speak and to hear the truth plainly and in a spirit of love.

HARRIET BEECHER STOWE

Don't make yourself a mouse, or the cat will eat you.

Necessity, my friend, is the mother of courage, as of invention.

We know what happens to people who stay in
the middle of the road. They get run over.

ANEURIN BEVAN

This will remain the land of the free only so long as
it is the home of the brave.

If it is thought that justice is with us, it
will give birth to courage.

ELMER DAVIS

We could never learn to be brave and patient, if
there were only joy in the world.

To sit by in silence, when they should protest, makes cowards
of men.

ABRAHAM LINCOLN

Physical bravery is an animal instinct; moral bravery is a much
higher and truer courage.

Heroism consists in hanging on one minute longer.

It often requires more courage to dare to do right
than to fear to do wrong.

ABRAHAM LINCOLN

Even cowards can endure hardships; only
the brave can endure suspense.

MIGNON MCLAUGHLIN

Courage is doing what you're afraid to do.
There can be no courage unless you're scared.

EDWARD V. RICKENBACKER

Tyranny, like hell, is not easily conquered; yet
we have this consolation with us, that the harder the conflict
the more glorious the triumph.

THOMAS PAINE

Flatterers are cats that lick before and scratch behind.

Bravery is the capacity to perform properly even
when scared half to death.

GENERAL OMAR BRADLEY

It is easy to be brave from a safe distance.

It is better to die in battle than to die of hunger.

The tiny ant dares to enter the lion's ear.

If you are an anvil, bear the strokes, and
if you become a hammer, strike.

Success is never final; failure is never fatal; it
is courage that counts.

WINSTON CHURCHILL

One man with courage is a majority.

ANDREW JACKSON

Living at risk is jumping off the cliff and
building your wings on the way down.

RAY BRADBURY

Never confuse a single defeat with a final defeat.

F. SCOTT FITZGERALD

Courage is bearing one's own personal tragedies without
dramatizing them to others.

WILLIAM FEATHER

In order to find the edge, you must risk going over the edge.

DENNIS DUGAN

Only those who dare to fail greatly can ever achieve greatly.

ROBERT F. KENNEDY

[Courage is] grace under pressure.

ERNEST HEMINGWAY

Money lost, nothing lost; courage lost, everything lost.

We are face to face with our destiny, and we must meet it with a high and resolute courage. For us is the life of action, of strenuous performance of duty; let us live in the harness, striving mightily; let us rather run the risk of wearing out than rusting out.

THEODORE ROOSEVELT

DETERMINATION

Keep on going, and the chances are
that you will stumble on something,
perhaps when you are least expecting it.
I have never heard of anyone stumbling
on something sitting down.

CHARLES F. KETTERING

Most of the trouble in the world is caused by
people wanting to be important.

T. S. ELIOT

Most people would succeed in small things, if
they were not troubled with great ambitions.

HENRY W. LONGFELLOW

Sometimes mere words are not enough—discipline is needed.
For words may not be heeded.

Always rise from the table with an appetite, and you will
never sit down without one.

WILLIAM PENN

Every beginning is difficult.

Failure is the opportunity to begin again more intelligently.

HENRY FORD

Don't waste energy trying to cover up failure. Learn
from your failures and go on to the next challenge.
It's OK to fail. If you're not failing, you're not growing.

H. STANLEY JUDD

I cannot give you the formula for success, but
I can give you the formula for failure . . . which is:
Try to please everybody.

HERBERT BAYARD SWOPE

When one must, one can.

If a man hasn't discovered something that
he will die for, he isn't fit to live.

MARTIN LUTHER KING JR.

Someday I hope to enjoy enough of what the world calls success so that somebody will ask me, "What's the secret of it?" I
shall say simply this: "I get up when I fall down."

PAUL HARVEY

If we are forced to fight, we must have the means and the
determination to prevail or we will not have what it takes to
secure the peace.

RONALD REAGAN

To him who is determined it remains only to act.

The anvil lasts longer than the hammer.

By constantly asking, one can reach China.

Courteous asking breaks even city walls.

Whatever you give your attention to
is the thing that governs your life.

Don't forget to swing hard, in case you hit the ball.

WOODIE HELD

All beginnings are difficult.

THE TALMUD

The first blow is as good as two.

A burden of one's own choice is not felt.

A good cause makes a stout heart and a strong arm.

You gotta play the hand that's dealt you.
There may be pain in that hand, but you play it.
And I've played it.

JAMES BRADY

The nearer any disease approaches to a crisis, the
nearer it is to a cure. Danger and deliverance make their
advances together, and it is only in the last push that one
or the other takes the lead.

THOMAS PAINE

If my doctor told me I only had six minutes to live, I
wouldn't brood. I'd type a little faster.

ISAAC ASIMOV

Nothing great was ever achieved without enthusiasm.

RALPH WALDO EMERSON

In things pertaining to enthusiasm, no man is sane who
does not know how to be insane on proper occasions.

HENRY WARD BEECHER

The great pleasure in life is doing what people say
you cannot do.

WALTER BAGEHOT

The greatest accomplishment is not in never falling, but
in rising again after you fall.

VINCE LOMBARDI

I have not yet begun to fight.

JOHN PAUL JONES

A fly can drive away horses.

Clearly define for yourself the long-range goals you aspire to,
and you will find that all the obstacles in your way will
become hills instead of mountains.

If you have an important point to make, don't
try to be subtle or clever. Use a pile driver.
Hit the point once. Then come back and hit it again.
Then hit it a third time—a tremendous whack.

WINSTON CHURCHILL

If I miss practicing on the piano one day, I can tell
the difference in my playing.
If I miss practicing on the piano for two days, my friends
can tell the difference. But if I miss the practice for
three days, my audience can tell the difference.

JAN PADEREWSKI

While attempting to invent the incandescent lamp, Thomas
Edison remarked after the 187th failure,
"We are making progress. Now, at least, we
know 187 things that won't work."

Do not pray for easy lives. Pray to be stronger men!
Do not pray for tasks equal to your powers.
Pray for powers equal to your tasks.

PHILLIPS BROOKS

I wish to preach, not the doctrine of ignoble ease, but
the doctrine of the strenuous life.

THEODORE ROOSEVELT

It takes twenty years to be an overnight success.

EDDIE CANTOR

The secret of success is constancy of purpose.

BENJAMIN DISRAELI

I have learned that success is to be measured not so much by
the position that one has reached in life as by the obstacles
which he has overcome while trying to succeed.

BOOKER T. WASHINGTON

When a man succeeds, he does it in spite of everybody, and
not with the assistance of everybody.

EDGAR WATSON HOWE

Success is counted sweetest
By those who ne'er succeed.

EMILY DICKINSON

Success: A subtle contrivance of Nature for
bringing about a man's defeat.

ELBERT HUBBARD

Success is a journey, not a destination.

BEN SWEETLAND

The key to executive success is the ability to
inspire teamwork.

HENRY L. DOHERTY

The difference between failure and success is
doing a thing nearly right and doing a thing exactly right.

EDWARD SIMMONS

The people who succeed are the few who have the ambition
and the willpower to develop themselves.

HERBERT CASSON

It is only as we develop others that we permanently succeed.

HARVEY S. FIRESTONE

Anybody can become a success in America if he's willing
to work while everybody else is killing time.

All it takes to be successful today is a willingness to start an
eight-hour day immediately after you finish the first one.

Nothing can be more hurtful to the service than
the neglect of discipline; for that discipline, more
than numbers, gives one army the superiority over another.

GEORGE WASHINGTON

Triumph—umph added to try.

It is not the critic who counts; not the man who points out how
the strong man stumbles, or where the doer of deeds could have
done them better. The credit belongs to the man who is actually
in the arena, whose face is marred by dust and sweat and blood;
who strives valiantly; who errs, and comes short again and again,
because there is no effort without error and shortcoming; but who
does actually strive to do the deeds; who knows the great enthusi-
asms, the great devotions; who spends himself in a worthy cause;
who at the best knows in the end the triumph of high achievement, and who at the worst, if he fails, at least fails while daring
greatly, so that his place shall never be with those cold and timid
souls who know neither victory nor defeat.

THEODORE ROOSEVELT

According to the theory of aerodynamics, as may be readily demonstrated through wind tunnel experiments, the bumblebee is unable to fly. This is because the size, weight, and shape of his body in relation to the total wingspread make flying impossible. But the bumblebee, being ignorant of these scientific truths, goes ahead and flies anyway—and makes a little honey every day.

RALPH L. WOODS

Make no little plans; they have no magic to stir men's blood and probably themselves will not be realized. Make big plans; aim high in hope and work, remembering that a noble, logical diagram once recorded will never die, but long after we are gone will be a living thing, asserting itself with ever-growing insistency. Remember that your sons and grandsons are going to do things that would stagger us. Let your watchword be order and your beacon beauty.

DANIEL H. BURNHAM

DILIGENCE

Few things are impossible to diligence
and skill . . . Great works are performed,
not by strength, but perseverance.

SAMUEL JOHNSON

The busy man has few idle visitors; to
the boiling pot the flies come not.

BENJAMIN FRANKLIN

With regard to ham and eggs: The chicken is involved; the
pig is committed.

ABRAHAM LINCOLN

Look for your choices, pick the best one, then go with it.

PAT RILEY

Small deeds done are better than great deeds planned.

GENERAL GEORGE C. MARSHALL

Drop by drop wears away the stone.

There is no royal road to anything. One thing at a time, all
things in succession. That which grows fast withers as rapidly;
that which grows slowly endures.

Good enough is the enemy of excellence.

Every job is a self-portrait of the person who did it.
Autograph your work with excellence.

We will be victorious if we have not forgotten how to learn.

ROSA LXEMBURG

Nothing in education is so astonishing as the amount of
ignorance it accumulates in the form of inert facts.

HENRY ADAMS

In the first place, God made idiots.
This was for practice. Then he made school boards.

MARK TWAIN

The chief wonder of education is that it does not ruin
everybody concerned in it, teachers and taught.

HENRY ADAMS

Swallow all your learning in the morning, but
digest it in company in the evening.

LORD CHESTERFIELD

He was so learned that he could name a horse in
nine languages; so ignorant that he bought a cow to ride on.

BENJAMIN FRANKLIN

A learned blockhead is a greater blockhead than
an ignorant one.

BENJAMIN FRANKLIN

They say that we are better educated than
our parents' generation.
What they mean is that we go to school longer.
They are not the same thing.

DOUGLAS YATES

He might be a very clever man by nature, for
all I know, but he laid so many books upon his head that
his brains could not move.

ROBERT HALL

I'm still waiting for some college to come up with a march
protesting student ignorance.

PAUL LARMER

Very few people can stand the strain of being educated
without getting superior over it.

STEPHEN LEACOCK

A man who has never gone to school may steal from
a freight car; but if he has a university education, he
may steal the whole railroad.

THEODORE ROOSEVELT

Education is something you get when your father sends
you to college. But it isn't complete until you send
your son there.

WASHINGTON JOURNAL

Give a man a fish, and you feed him for a day.
Teach a man to fish and you feed him for a lifetime.

CHINESE PROVERB

Experience keeps a dear school, but fools will learn in no other.

To educate a man in mind and not in morals is to educate a
menace to society.

THEODORE ROOSEVELT

Upon the subject of education, not presuming to dictate any plan
or system respecting it, I can only say that I view it as the most
important subject which we, as a people, can be engaged in.

ABRAHAM LINCOLN

Do the duty that lies nearest thee; thy
next duty will then become clearer.

GOETHE

He that performs his own errand saves the messenger's hire.

Experience is a good teacher, but she sends in terrific bills.

MINNA ANTRIM

Experience is the best of schoolmasters, only
the school fees are heavy.

THOMAS CARLYLE

Experience is the name everyone gives to his mistakes.

OSCAR WILDE

I have but one lamp by which my feet are guided, and
that is the lamp of experience. I know of no way of judging
the future but by the past.

PATRICK HENRY

Experience teaches you to recognize a mistake when
you've made it again.

He that waits upon fortune is never sure of a dinner.

BENJAMIN FRANKLIN

Well done is better than well said.

BENJAMIN FRANKLIN

Do something every day that you don't want to do; this
is the golden rule for acquiring the habit of
doing your duty without pain.

MARK TWAIN

Act well your part; there all the honor lies.
He who does something at the head of one regiment, will
eclipse him who does nothing at the head of a hundred.

ABRAHAM LINCOLN

Let us have faith that right makes might, and in that faith let us to the end dare to do our duty as we understand it.

ABRAHAM LINCOLN

I do the very best I know how—the very best I can; and I mean to keep doing so until the end. If the end brings me out all right, what is said against me won't amount to anything. If the end brings me out wrong, ten angels swearing I was right would make no difference. What you can't get out of, get into wholeheartedly.

MIGNON MCLAUGHLIN

For want of a nail, the shoe was lost; for want of a shoe the horse was lost; and for want of a horse the rider was lost, being over-taken and slain by the enemy, all for want of care about a horseshoe nail.

BENJAMIN FRANKLIN

Let no guilty man escape if it can be avoided. Be specially vigi-lant—or instruct those engaged in the prosecution of fraud to be against all who insinuate that they have high influence to protect—or to protect them. No personal consideration should stand in the way of performing a public duty.

ULYSSES S. GRANT

Duties are not performed for duty's sake, but because their neglect would make the man uncomfortable. A man performs but one duty—the duty of contenting his spirit, the duty of making himself agreeable to himself.

MARK TWAIN

An education isn't how much you have committed to memory, or even how much you know. It's being able to differentiate between what you do know and what you don't. It's knowing where to go to find out what you need to know; and it's know-ing how to use the information you get.

WILLIAM FEATHER

There is no evil that we cannot either face or fly from, but the consciousness of duty disregarded. A sense of duty pursues us ever. It is omnipresent, like the Deity. If we take to ourselves the wings of the morning, and dwell in the uttermost parts of the sea, duty performed or duty violated is still with us, for our happiness or our misery. If we say the darkness shall cover us, in the darkness as in the light our obligations are yet with us.

DANIEL WEBSTER

Duty is the sublimest word in our language.
Do your duty in all things. You cannot do more.
You should never wish to do less.

FAMILY

At the end only two things really
matter to a man, regardless of who he
is; and they are the affection and
understanding of his family.
Anything and everything else he
creates is insubstantial; they are
ships given over to the mercy of the
winds and tides of prejudice.

RICHARD E. BYRD

Cleaning your house while your kids are still growing is
like shoveling the walk before it stops snowing.

PHYLLIS DILLER

I come from a wealthy family.
My brother is worth fifty thousand dollars—dead or alive.

A distant relative is one who recently
borrowed money from you.

I don't have to look up my family tree because I
know that I'm the sap.

FRED ALLEN

We pay for the mistakes of our ancestors, and it seems only
fair that they should leave us the money to pay with.

DON MARQUIS

The best blood will sometimes get into a fool or a mosquito.

AUSTIN O'MALLEY

Many kiss the child for the nurse's sake.

JOHN HEYWOOD

Generally when a man brags about his pedigree
he has nothing else to brag about.

REFLECTIONS OF A BACHELOR

There are no real difficulties in a home where
the children hope to be like their parents one day.

WILLIAM LYON PHELPS

Better to be driven out from among men than
to be disliked of children.

RICHARD HENRY DANA

You can do anything with children if
you only play with them.

OTTO VON BISMARCK

Men are generally more careful of the breed of their horses
and dogs than of their children.

WILLIAM PENN

When I was a kid my parents moved a lot—but
I always found them.

RODNEY DANGERFIELD

I know a lot about children.
Not being an author, I'm a great critic.

FINLEY PETER DUNNE

Teach your child to hold his tongue; he'll
learn fast enough to speak.

BENJAMIN FRANKLIN

Before I got married, I had six theories about
bringing up children; now I have six children and no theories.

LORD ROCHESTER

The children now love luxury; they have bad manners, contempt for authority; they show disrespect for elders and love chatter in place of exercise. Children are now tyrants, not the servants of their households. They no longer rise when elders enter the room. They contradict their parents, chatter before company, gobble up dainties at the table, cross their legs, and tyrannize their teachers.

SOCRATES

Every child should have an occasional pat on the back as long as it is applied low enough and hard enough.

BISHOP FULTON J. SHEEN

The thing that impresses me most about America is the way parents obey their children.

DUKE OF WINDSOR

I've seen kids ride bicycles, run, play ball, set up a camp, swing, fight a war, swim, and race for eight hours . . . yet have to be driven to the garbage can.

ERMA BOMBECK

Oh, what a tangled web do parents weave when they think that their children are naive.

OGDEN NASH

Ask your child what he wants for dinner only if he's buying.

FRAN LEBOWITZ

Children are poor men's riches.

One cannot see the evil deeds of one's own children.

Small children give you headache; big children, heartache.

When children stand still, they have done some ill.

Vacation time is when kids get out of school
and into your hair.

To train a child properly, start at the bottom.

Child psychology is what children manage parents with.

Children are often spoiled because you can't
spank two grandmothers.

He who takes the child by the hand takes the mother
by the heart.

The young always have the same problem: how to rebel
and conform at the same time.
They have now solved this by defying their parents
and copying one another.
QUENTIN CRISP

There's only one pretty child in the world, and
every mother has it.

With a child in the house, all corners are full.

Children seldom misquote you . . . they repeat
what you shouldn't have said word for word.

Two of anything but children make a pair; two
of them make a mob.

The most influential of all educational factors is
the conversation in a child's home.
WILLIAM TEMPLE

Eye contact is crucial not only in making good communicational contact with a child, but in filling his emotional needs. Without realizing it, we use eye contact as a primary means of conveying love, especially to children. A child uses eye contact with his parents (and others) to feed emotionally. The more parents make eye contact with their child as a means of expressing their love, the more a child is nourished with love and the fuller is his emotional tank.

ROSS CAMPBELL

Tell me who your father is, and I'll tell you who you are.

Let every father remember that one day his son will follow his example instead of his advice.

NUGGETS

The most important thing a father can do for his children is to love their mother.

THEODORE M. HESBURGH

No man is responsible for his father. That is entirely his mother's affair.

MARGARET TURNBULL

Men who are ashamed of the way their fathers made their money are never ashamed to spend it.

If you would civilize a man, begin with his grandmother.

VICTOR HUGO

A grandmother is a mother who has a second chance.

Almost every grandparent will tell you that spanking is unnecessary for your children, even though it was felt necessary for you.

If a man is fortunate he will, before he dies, gather
up as much as he can of his civilized heritage and
transmit it to his children.

WILL DURANT

Every time I hear a person say that his home life is
unbearable I wonder if I'm not listening to the bear.

No nation can be destroyed while it possesses
a good home life.

JOSIAH GILBERT HOLLAND

I long for rural and domestic scenes, for the
warbling of birds and the prattle of my children . . . As
much as I converse with sages or heroes, they have
very little of my love or admiration. I should prefer the
delights of a garden to the dominion of a world.

JOHN ADAMS

A home is ruled by the sickest person in it.

NITZBERG'S OBSERVATION

Nostalgia is longing for the place you wouldn't move back to.

The honeymoon is over when the dog brings
your slippers and your wife barks at you.

Travel east or travel west, a man's own house is still the best.

Housework is something you do that nobody
notices unless you don't do it.

The first thing a woman should do to make a successful husband out of a man is admire him.

All husbands are alike, but they have different faces
so you can tell them apart.

I may be old-fashioned, but I expect my wife
to help me with the dishes.

When I was a young man, I vowed never to marry until I
found the ideal woman. Well, I found her—but alas, she was
waiting for the ideal man.

ROBERT SCHUMANN

One of the greatest joys is to have grandchildren fight
over your lap.

I kiss my kids "good night" no matter how late I have
to wait up for them.

A happy marriage is a long conversation that
seems all too short.

ANDRE MAUROIS

Successful marriage is always a triangle: a man, a
woman, and God.

T. CECIL MYERS

In marriage it is all very well to say that
"the two are made one." The question is: Which one?

A marriage is like a long trip in a tiny rowboat: If
one passenger starts to rock the boat, the other has to
steady it; otherwise they will go to the bottom together.

DAVID REUBEN

Marriage is like twirling a baton, turning handsprings, or
eating with chopsticks. It looks easy till you try it.

After a few years of marriage, a man can look right at a woman without seeing her—and a woman can see right through a man without looking at him.

HELEN ROWLAND

Before marriage the three little words are "I love you"; after marriage they are "Let's eat out."

The most difficult years of marriage are those following the wedding.

Before marriage a man will lie awake all night thinking about something you said; after marriage he'll fall asleep before you finish saying it.

HELEN ROWLAND

Don't marry for money; you can borrow it cheaper.

SCOTTISH PROVERB

Nowadays two can live as cheaply as one large family used to!

JOEY ADAMS

My wife and I made a bargain many years ago that in order to live harmoniously, I would decide all the major problems and she would decide all the unimportant problems. So far, in our twenty-five years of matrimony, we have never had any major problems.

JUDGE JONAH GOLDSTEIN

Marriage is a lottery, but you can't tear up your ticket if you lose.

F. M. KNOWLES

Many a man in love with a dimple makes the mistake of marrying the whole girl.

STEPHEN LEACOCK

The Japanese have a word for it. It's "judo"—the art of
conquering by yielding.
The Western equivalent of judo is "Yes, dear."

J. P. MCEVOY

Marriages are made in heaven—so is thunder and lightning.

A good marriage would be between a blind wife
and a deaf husband.

MICHEL DE MONTAIGNE

It resembles a pair of shears, so joined that they
cannot be separated, often moving in opposite directions, yet
always punishing anyone who comes between them.

SYDNEY SMITH

We sleep in separate rooms; we have dinner apart; we
take separate vacations—we're doing everything we can to
keep our marriage together.

RODNEY DANGERFIELD

Only choose in marriage a woman whom you would
choose as a friend if she were a man.

JOSEPH JOUBERT

Marriage is not just spiritual communion and passionate
embraces; marriage is also three meals a day and
remembering to carry out the trash.

DR. JOYCE BROTHERS

Success in marriage is much more than finding the right person; it is a matter of being the right person.

BARNETT ROBERT BRICKNER

All marriages are happy.
It's the living together afterward that causes all the trouble.

Often the difference between a successful marriage and a
mediocre one consists of leaving about three or four things a
day unsaid.

HARLAN MILLER

It is a sorry house in which the cock is silent
and the hen crows.

It's a formal wedding when the shotgun is painted white.

Soon after a man gets married he starts losing the
space originally assigned to him in the bedroom clothes closet.

My mother taught me not only the three R's, but
she implanted in my mind the love and purpose of learning.
My mother was the making of me.
She understood me; she let me follow my bents.

THOMAS EDISON

To see a young couple loving each other is no wonder; but
to see an old couple loving each other is the best sight of all.

WILLIAM M. THACKERAY

One of the greatest pleasures a parent can experience is to
gaze upon the children when they're fast asleep.

Nothing annoys the average child today like
a disobedient parent.

If parents would worry more about when their children turn
in, they'd have to worry less about how they'll turn out.

The easiest way to get your son to follow in your footsteps
today is to offer him the keys to your car.

If your children spend most of their time in other people's houses, you're lucky; if they all congregate at your house, you're blessed.

Grown-ups never understand anything for themselves, and it is tiresome for children to be always and forever explaining things to them.

ANTOINE DE SAINT-EXUPERY

I have thought about it a great deal, and the more I think, the more certain I am that obedience is the gateway through which knowledge, yes, and love, too, enter the mind of a child.

ANNIE SULLIVAN (TEACHER OF HELEN KELLER)

The trouble with many hands that rock the cradle today is that they're hired hands.

"Leisure" is the two minutes' rest a man gets while his wife is thinking up something else for him to do.

Insanity is hereditary. You can get it from your children.

SAM LEVENSON

Wait! Wait! To children it seems this is all they hear. Yet the very act of waiting is valuable training, for waiting is something they will have to do all their lives. The youth must wait for his right to drive a car, the student for his diploma, the lawyer for his degree, the worker for the salary increase, the married couple for the home they want. Teaching a child to wait is just as important as the training in manners and morals that he receives at his mother's knee.

DOROTHY BRANT WARRICK

"A house without books is like a room without windows. No man has a right to bring up his children without surrounding them with books. Children learn to read by being in the presence of books. The love of knowledge comes with reading and grows upon it." Although modern educators may regard that as somewhat old-fashioned, or as an oversimplification, they do still surround children with books, and they strive to create in the young the desire to read not only for knowledge and for the tools of thinking but also for sheer enjoyment.

HORACE MANN

FORGIVENESS

Sometimes we find it hard to forgive.
We forget that forgiveness is as much for
us as for the other person. If you can't
forgive it's like holding a hot coal in your
hand—you're the one getting burned.
The tension may be hurting you much more
than the other person.

JENNIFER JAMES

'Tis more noble to forgive, and more manly to despise, than
to revenge an injury.

If we are bound to forgive an enemy, we are not
bound to trust him.

It is very easy to forgive others their mistakes.
It takes more guts and gumption to forgive them
for having witnessed your own.

JESSAMYN WEST

Doing an injury puts you below your enemy; revenging
one makes you but even with him; forgiving
it sets you above him.

BENJAMIN FRANKLIN

It is easier to forgive an enemy than to forgive a friend.

WILLIAM BLAKE

Be kind and compassionate to one another, forgiving
each other, just as in Christ God forgave you.

EPHESIANS 4:32

Everyone says forgiveness is a lovely idea, until
they have something to forgive.

C. S. LEWIS

Always forgive your enemies—nothing annoys them so much.

OSCAR WILDE

He that cannot forgive others breaks the bridge over which he
must pass himself; for every man has need to be forgiven.

THOMAS FULLER

Forgiveness is the fragrance the violet sheds on
the heel that has crushed it.

MARK TWAIN

There's no point in burying a hatchet if
you're going to put up a marker on the site.

SYDNEY HARRIS

Forgiveness is not a feeling but a promise or commitment to the
following three things:
1. I will not use it against them in the future.
2. I will not talk to others about them.
3. I will not dwell on it myself.

JAY E. ADAMS

One pardons in the degree that one loves.

LA ROCHEFOUCAULD

To understand is to forgive.

FRENCH PROVERB

Don't carry a grudge. While you're carrying the grudge the
other guy's out dancing.

BUDDY HACKETT

The weak can never forgive.
Forgiveness is the attribute of the strong.

GANDHI

Forgive your enemies, but never forget their names.

JOHN F. KENNEDY

We can forgive almost anything except
the person who has to forgive us.

Write injuries in dust, benefits in marble.

BENJAMIN FRANKLIN

Clara Barton, founder of the American Red Cross, was once
reminded of an especially cruel thing that had been done to her
years before. But Miss Barton seemed not to recall it. "Don't you
remember it?" her friend asked. "No," came the reply, "I distinctly remember forgetting the incident."

SUNSHINE MAGAZINE

FREEDOM

Freedom is still expensive. It still
costs money. It still costs blood. It
still calls for courage and endurance,
not only in soldiers, but in every man
and woman who is free and who is
determined to remain free.

HARRY S. TRUMAN

The merchants will manage the better, the more
they are left free to manage for themselves.

Better to die upright than to live on your knees.

You're a grand old flag; you're a high-flying flag; and forever,
in peace, may you wave. You're the emblem of the land I love,
the home of the free and the brave . . .

GEORGE M. COHAN

Our flag has never waved over any community but in blessing.

WILLIAM McKINLEY

Liberty is the one thing you cannot love unless
you are willing to give it to others.

WILLIAM ALLEN WHITE

God grants liberty only to those who love it and
are always ready to guard and defend it.

DANIEL WEBSTER

Our reliance is in the love of liberty which God has planted in
us. Our defense is in the spirit which prizes liberty as the heritage of all men, in all lands everywhere.

ABRAHAM LINCOLN

The inescapable price of liberty is an ability to preserve it from destruction.

DOUGLAS MACARTHUR

Liberty means responsibility. That is why most men dread it.

GEORGE BERNARD SHAW

The things required for prosperous labor, prosperous manufactures, and prosperous commerce are three. First, liberty; second, liberty; third, liberty.

HENRY WARD BEECHER

Liberty is always dangerous, but it is the safest thing we have.

HENRY EMERSON FOSDICK

Our union is now complete; our constitution composed, established and approved. You are now the guardians of your own liberties.

SAMUEL ADAMS

Liberty, when it begins to take root, is a plant of rapid growth.

GEORGE WASHINGTON

Liberty is the proper end and object of authority, and cannot subsist without it; and it is a liberty to that only which is good, just, and honest.

JOHN WINTHROP

Those who would give up essential liberty to purchase a little temporary safety deserve neither liberty nor safety.

BENJAMIN FRANKLIN

The true danger is when liberty is nibbled away, for expedients, and by parts.

EDMUND BURKE

True liberty consists only in the power of doing
what we ought to will, and in not being constrained
to do what we ought not to will.

JONATHAN EDWARDS

The tree of liberty must be refreshed from time to time with
the blood of patriots and tyrants.
It is its natural manure.

THOMAS JEFFERSON

Let every nation know, whether it wishes us well
or ill, that we shall pay any price, bear any burden, meet
any hardship, support any friend, oppose any foe
to assure the survival and the success of liberty.

JOHN F. KENNEDY

He that would make his own liberty secure must
guard even his enemy from oppression.

THOMAS PAINE

The history of liberty is a history of resistance.
The history of liberty is a history of the limitation of
governmental power, not the increase of it.

WOODROW WILSON

I would remind you that extremism in the defense of
liberty is no vice. And let me remind you also
that moderation in the pursuit of justice is no virtue.

BARRY GOLDWATER

No people ever lost their liberties unless
they themselves first became corrupt.
The people are the safeguards of their own liberties, and
I rely wholly on them to guard themselves.

ANDREW JACKSON

When liberty is taken away by force, it can be
restored by force. When it is relinquished voluntarily
by default, it can never be recovered.

DOROTHY THOMPSON

Liberty exists in proportion to wholesome restraint; the
more restraint on others to keep off from us, the
more liberty we have.

DANIEL WEBSTER

I would rather belong to a poor nation that was free than to a
rich nation that had ceased to be in love with liberty.
We shall not be poor if we love liberty.

WOODROW WILSON

It is a common observation here that our cause is the cause of
all mankind, and that we are fighting for their liberty in
defending our own.

BENJAMIN FRANKLIN

Give me your tired, your poor,
Your huddled masses yearning to breathe free,
The wretched refuse of your teeming shore;
Send these, the homeless, tempest-tossed to me.
I lift my lamp beside the golden door!

EMMA LAZARUS

Eternal vigilance is the price of liberty.

WENDELL PHILLIPS

A free people ought not only to be armed, but disciplined.

GEORGE WASHINGTON

When good people in any country cease their vigilance and
struggle, then evil men prevail.

PEARL BUCK

Human freedom is not a gift of man. It is an achievement by man; and, as it was gained by vigilance and struggle, so it may be lost in indifference and supineness.

HARRY F. BYRD

For a people who are free, and who mean to remain so, a well-organized and armed militia is their best security.

THOMAS JEFFERSON

Our institutions of freedom will not survive unless they are constantly replenished by the faith that gave them birth.

JOHN FOSTER DULLES

Freedom means self-expression, and the secret of freedom is courage. No man ever remains free who acquiesces in what he knows to be wrong.

HAROLD J. LASKI

Those who deny freedom to others deserve it not for themselves. And, under a just God, cannot long retain it.

ABRAHAM LINCOLN

For what avail the plow or sail,
Or land or life, if freedom fail?

RALPH WALDO EMERSON

The greatest glory of a freeborn people is to transmit that freedom to their children.

WILLIAM HARVARD

Those who expect to reap the blessings of freedom must, like men, undergo the fatigues of supporting it.

THOMAS PAINE

Most men have a tendency to imprison themselves—without the help of the authorities.

HENRY MILLER

Let freedom never perish in your hands, but
piously transmit it to your children.

JOSEPH ADDISON

Everything can be taken from a man but one thing: the
last of human freedoms—to choose one's attitude
in any given set of circumstances—to
choose one's own way.

VIKTOR FRANKEL

I intend no modification of my oft-expressed personal wish
that all men everywhere could be free.

ABRAHAM LINCOLN

There can be no greater good than the quest for peace, and
no finer purpose than the preservation of freedom.

RONALD REAGAN

Without freedom of thought, there can be no such thing
as wisdom; and no such thing as public liberty, without
freedom of speech.

BENJAMIN FRANKLIN

No man is entitled to the blessings of freedom unless
he be vigilant in its preservation.

DOUGLAS MACARTHUR

With malice toward none, with charity for all, with firmness in
the right, as God gives us to see the right, let us strive on to finish the work we are in, to bind up the nation's wounds, to care
for him who shall have borne the battle and for his widow and
his orphan, to do all which may achieve and cherish a just and
lasting peace among ourselves and with all nations.

ABRAHAM LINCOLN

But the character of every act depends upon the circumstances in which it is done. The most stringent protection of free speech would not protect a man in falsely shouting fire in a theater and causing a panic. It does not even protect a man from an injunction against uttering words that may have all the effect of force. The question in every case is whether the words used are used in such circumstances and are of such a nature as to create a clear and present danger that they will bring about the substantive evils that . . . Congress has a right to prevent. It is a question of proximity and degree.

OLIVER WENDELL HOLMES

For if men are to be precluded from offering their sentiments on a matter, which may involve the most serious and alarming consequences, that can invite the consideration of mankind, reason is of no use to us; the freedom of speech may be taken away, and, dumb and silent we may be led, like sheep, to the slaughter.

GEORGE WASHINGTON

I have always been among those who believed that the greatest freedom of speech was the greatest safety, because if a man is a fool, the best thing to do is to encourage him to advertise the fact by speaking. It cannot be so easily discovered if you allow him to remain silent and look wise, but if you let him speak, the secret is out, and the world knows that he is a fool. So it is by the exposure of folly that it is defeated; not by the seclusion of folly, and in this free air of free speech men get into that sort of communication with one another which constitutes the basis of all common achievement.

What is necessary for the use of land is not its private ownership, but the security of improvements. It is not necessary to say to a man, "This land is yours," in order to induce him to cultivate or improve it. It is only necessary to say to him, "Whatever your labor or capital produces on this land shall be yours."

HENRY GEORGE

Is the relinquishment of the trial by jury and the liberty of the press necessary for your liberty? Will the abandonment of your most sacred rights tend to the security of your liberty? Liberty, the greatest of all earthly blessings—give us that precious jewel, and you may take everything else! Guard with jealous attention the public liberty. Suspect everyone who approaches that jewel.

PATRICK HENRY

There is a just God who presides over the destinies of nations and who will raise up friends to fight our battles for us. The battle, sir, is not to the strong alone; it is to the vigilant, the active, the brave. It is vain, sir, to extenuate the matter. Gentlemen may cry, peace, peace—but there is no peace. The war is actually begun! The next gale that sweeps from the north will bring to our ears the clash of resounding arms! Our brethren are already in the field! Why stand we here idle? What is it that gentlemen wish? What would they have? Is life so dear, or peace so sweet, as to be purchased at the price of chains and slavery? Forbid it, almighty God! I know not what course others may take; but as for me, give me liberty, or give me death!

PATRICK HENRY

The whole history of the progress of human liberty shows that all concessions yet made to her august claims have been made of earnest struggle. If there is no struggle, there is no progress. Those who profess to favor freedom yet deprecate agitation, are men who want crops without plowing up the ground; they want rain without thunder and lightning. They want the ocean without the awful roar of its many waters. Power concedes nothing without a demand. It never did and it never will. The limits of tyrants are prescribed by the endurance of those whom they oppress.

FREDERICK DOUGLASS

The spirit of liberty is the spirit which is not too sure that it is right; the spirit of liberty is the spirit which seeks to understand the minds of other men and women; the spirit of liberty is the spirit which weighs their interests alongside its own without bias; the spirit of liberty remembers that not even a sparrow falls to earth unheeded; the spirit of liberty is the spirit of Him who, near two thousand years ago, taught mankind that lesson it has never learned, but has never quite forgotten: that here is a kingdom where the least shall be heard and considered side by side with the greatest.

LEARNED HAND

Eternal vigilance is the price of liberty; power is ever stealing from the many to the few. The manna of popular liberty must be gathered each day, or it is rotten. The living sap of today outgrows the dead rind of yesterday. The hand entrusted with power becomes, either from human depravity or esprit de corps, the necessary enemy of the people. Only by continued oversight can the democrat in office be prevented from hardening into a despot; only by unintermitted agitation can a people be sufficiently awake to principle not to let liberty be smothered in material prosperity.

WENDELL PHILLIPS

If the true spark of religious and civil liberty be kindled, it will burn. Human agency cannot extinguish it. Like the earth's central fire, it may be smothered for a time; the ocean may overwhelm it; mountains may press it down; but its inherent and unconquerable force will heave both the ocean and the land, and at some time or other, in some place or other, the volcano will break out and flame up to heaven.

DANIEL WEBSTER

But we know that freedom cannot be served by the devices of the tyrant. As it is an ancient truth that freedom cannot be legislated into existence, so it is no less obvious that freedom cannot be censored into existence. And any who act as if freedom's defenses are to be found in suppression and suspicion and fear confess a doctrine that is alien to America.

DWIGHT D. EISENHOWER

We in this country, in this generation, are—by destiny rather than choice—the watchmen on the walls of world freedom. We ask, therefore, that we may be worthy of our power and responsibility, that we may exercise our strength with wisdom and restraint, and that we may achieve in our time and for all time the ancient vision of "peace on earth, good will toward men." That must always be our goal, and the righteousness of our cause must always underlie our strength. For as was written long ago: "Except the Lord keep the city, the watchman waketh but in vain."

JOHN F. KENNEDY

Without an unfettered press, without liberty of speech, all the outward forms and structures of free institutions are a sham, a pretense—the sheerest mockery. If the press is not free; if speech is not independent and untrammeled; if the mind is shackled or made impotent through fear, it makes no difference under what form of government you live; you are a subject and not a citizen. Republics are not in and of themselves better than other forms of government except insofar as they carry with them and guarantee to the citizen that liberty of thought and action for which they were established.

WILLIAM E. BORAH

If the fires of freedom and civil liberties burn low in other lands, they must be made brighter in our own. If in other lands, the press and books and literature of all kinds are censored, we must redouble our efforts here to keep them free. If in other lands the eternal truths of the past are threatened by intolerance, we must provide a safe place for their perpetuation.

FRANKLIN D. ROOSEVELT

FRIENDSHIP

Without friends no one would choose
to live, though he had all other goods.

ARISTOTLE

A man is known by the company he keeps out of.

A. CRAIG

Who friendship with a knave has made
Is judged a partner in the trade.

JOHN GAY

To find a friend one must close one eye; to keep him, two.

NORMAN DOUGLAS

A true friend unbosoms freely, advises justly, assists readily,
adventures boldly, takes all patiently, defends courageously,
and continues a friend unchangeably.

WILLIAM PENN

Distance preserves friendship.

No enemy is more dangerous than a friend who isn't quite sure
he is for or against you.

Be slow in choosing a friend, slower in changing.

Anyone can sympathize with the sufferings of a friend, but
it requires a very fine nature to sympathize
with a friend's success.

OSCAR WILDE

"Stay" is a charming word in a friend's vocabulary.

AMOS BRONSON ALCOTT

Don't tell your friends their social faults; they will cure the fault and never forgive you.

LOGAN PEARSALL SMITH

To have a good enemy, choose a friend; he knows where to strike.

DIANE DE POITIERS

Little friends may prove great friends.

AESOP

Knock your friends often enough, and soon you'll find no one at home.

Choose your friends like your books: few but choice.

He who judges between two friends loses one of them.

One should go invited to a friend in good fortune and uninvited in misfortune.

Speak well of your friend; of your enemy say nothing.

Tell me who your friends are, and I'll tell you who you are.

A relationship is a living thing.
It needs and benefits from the same attention to detail that an artist lavishes on his art.

DAVID VISCOTT

Take time to be friendly. It is the road to happiness.

Friendship is like money: easier made than kept.

SAMUEL BUTLER

A friend is a present you give yourself.

Familiarity breeds contempt—and children.

MARK TWAIN

Friendship is only purchased with friendship.

Do not use a hatchet to remove a fly from
your friend's forehead.

CHINESE PROVERB

Santa Claus has the right idea: Visit people once a year.

VICTOR BORGE

Everybody forgets the basic thing:
People are not going to love you unless you love them.

PAT CARROLL

Never explain—your friends do not need it, and
your enemies will not believe you anyway.

ELBERT HUBBARD

True friendship is a plant of slow growth and must
undergo and withstand the shocks of adversity before
it is entitled to the appellation.

GEORGE WASHINGTON

The better part of one's life consists of his friendships.

ABRAHAM LINCOLN

GOD

No people can be bound to acknowledge
and adore the Invisible Hand which
conducts the affairs of men more than
those of the United States.

GEORGE WASHINGTON

Blessed is the nation whose God is the Lord.

PSALM 33:12

The God who gave us life, gave us liberty at the same time.

THOMAS JEFFERSON

Seek truth in all things.
God reveals Himself through the created world.

THOMAS AQUINAS

Sometimes a nation abolishes God, but
fortunately God is more tolerant.

HERBERT V. PROCHNOW

If we spend sixteen hours a day dealing with tangible things
and only five minutes a day dealing with God, is
it any wonder that tangible things are two hundred times
more real to us than God?

WILLIAM R. INGE

God is not a cosmic bellboy for whom we can press
a button to get things.

HARRY EMERSON FOSDICK

Don't stay away from church because there are
so many hypocrites. There's always room for one more.

A. R. ADAMS

I know that the Lord is always on the side of the right.
But it is my constant anxiety and prayer that I and
this nation should be on the Lord's side.

ABRAHAM LINCOLN

I believe in God in His wisdom and benevolence, and
I cannot conceive that such a Being could make
such a species as the human merely to live and die
on this earth. If I did not believe [in] a future state, I
should believe in no God.

JOHN ADAMS

The most successful men I know have always admitted that
they would most surely have failed without God's help.

To be like Christ is to be a Christian.

WILLIAM PENN

Whatever makes men good Christians makes
them good citizens.

DANIEL WEBSTER

Wherever God erects a house of prayer,
The devil always builds a chapel there;
And 'twill be found, upon examination,
The latter has the largest congregation.

DANIEL DEFOE

A great many more men would want to go to church
if there were a law against it.

Wherever there is a human being, I see God-given rights
inherent in the being, whatever may be the sex
or the complexion.

WILLIAM LLOYD GARRISON

An atheist is a man who has no invisible means of support.

JOHN BUCHAN

Government laws are needed to give us civil rights, and
God is needed to make us civil.

REVEREND RALPH W. SOCKMAN

I would advise no one to send his child where
the holy Scriptures are not supreme.
Every institution that does not unceasingly pursue the
study of God's word becomes corrupt.

MARTIN LUTHER

Work for the Lord. The pay is small, but
the retirement benefits are out of this world.

All I have seen teaches me to trust the Creator
for all I have not seen.

RALPH WALDO EMERSON

HERE IS MY CREED.
I believe in one God, creator of the universe.
That He governs it by his providence.
That He ought to be worshiped.
That the most acceptable service we render Him is doing
good to His other children.
That the soul of man is immortal and will be treated with jus-
tice in another life respecting its conduct in this.

BENJAMIN FRANKLIN

The sages and heroes of history are receding from us.
But time has no power over the name and deeds
and words of Jesus Christ.

WILLIAM ELLERY CHANNING

Of all kinds of knowledge that we can ever obtain, the
knowledge of God and the knowledge of ourselves
are the most important.

JONATHAN EDWARDS

Someone has tabulated that we have 35 million laws on the
books to enforce the Ten Commandments.

BERT MASTERSON

Often God has to shut a door in our face so that He can subse-
quently open the door through which He wants us to go.

CATHERINE MARSHALL

The Christian ministry is the worst of all trades, but
the best of all professions.

JOHN NEWTON

Still as of old, men by themselves are priced—
For thirty pieces Judas sold himself, not Christ.

HESTER H. CHOLMODELEY

Nothing is so fatal to religion as indifference, which
is, at least, half infidelity.

EDMUND BURKE

Men will wrangle for religion, write for it, fight for it, die
for it, anything but—live for it.

C. C. COLTON

The legislature of the United States shall pass no law
on the subject of religion nor touching or abridging
the liberty of the press.

CHARLES PINCKNEY

True repentance always involves reform.

HOSEA BALLOU

We don't call it sin today; we call it self-expression.

BARONESS STOCKS

We have grasped the mystery of the atom and rejected
the Sermon on the Mount.

GENERAL OMAR BRADLEY

Keep yourself from opportunity, and God
will keep you from sins.

JACOB CATS

Every sin is the result of a collaboration.

STEPHEN CRANE

Men are punished by their sins, not for them.

ELBERT HUBBARD

There is no sin committed without previous preparation.

Sin has always been an ugly word, but
it has been made so in a new sense over
the last half-century. It has been made not only ugly
but passé. People are no longer sinful, they
are only immature or
underprivileged or frightened or, more particularly, sick.

PHYLLIS MCGINLEY

Commit the oldest sins the newest kind of ways.

WILLIAM SHAKESPEARE

There is one inevitable criterion of judgment touching
religious faith in doctrinal matters.
Can you reduce it to practice? If not, have none of it.

HOSEA BALLOU

The Lord prefers common-looking people.
That is the reason He makes so many of them.

ABRAHAM LINCOLN

Beauty may be said to be God's trademark in creation.

HENRY WARD BEECHER

One, on God's side, is a majority.

WENDELL PHILLIPS

What good will it be for a man if he gains the whole world,
yet forfeits his soul?
Or what can a man give in exchange for his soul?

MATTHEW 16:26

God will not look you over for medals, degrees or diplomas,
but for scars.

ELBERT HUBBARD

The great act of faith is when man decides that he is not God.

OLIVER WENDELL HOLMES

But those who hope in the Lord will renew their strength.
They will soar on wings like eagles; they will run and
not grow weary; they will walk and not be faint.

ISAIAH 40:31

It is impossible to mentally or socially enslave
a Bible-reading people. The principles of the Bible are the
groundwork of human freedom.

HORACE GREELEY

Freedom will speak everywhere, and
its speech will be biblical.

HEINRICH HEINE

The Bible is a window in this prison-world, through
which we may look into eternity.

TIMOTHY DWIGHT

No man ever did or ever will become truly eloquent
without being a constant reader of the Bible, and
an admirer of the purity and sublimity of its language.

FISHER AMES

In regard to this great Book, I have but to say, it
is the best gift God has given to man.
All the good the Savior gave to the world
was communicated through this book.
But for it we could not know right from wrong.

ABRAHAM LINCOLN

The parents have a right to say
that no teacher paid by their money shall
rob their children of faith in God and
send them back to their homes skeptical or
infidels or agnostics or atheists.

WILLIAM JENNINGS BRYAN

Faith is an outward and visible sign of a
inward and spiritual grace.

It is more important to know that we are on God's side.

ABRAHAM LINCOLN

It is the duty of nations as well as of men to own their dependence upon the overruling power of God, to confess their sins
and transgressions in humble sorrow, yet with assured hope that
genuine repentance will lead to mercy and pardon.

ABRAHAM LINCOLN

THE TEN COMMANDMENTS

You shall have no other gods before me.

You shall not make for yourself an idol in the form of anything in heaven above or on the earth beneath or in the waters below. You shall not bow down to them or worship them; for I, the LORD your God, am a jealous God, punishing the children for the sin of the fathers to the third and fourth generation of those who hate me, but showing love to a thousand generations of those who love me and keep my commandments.

You shall not misuse the name of the LORD your God, for the LORD will not hold anyone guiltless who misuses his name.

Remember the Sabbath day by keeping it holy. Six days you shall labor and do all your work, but the seventh day is a Sabbath to the LORD your God. On it you shall not do any work, neither you, nor your son or daughter, nor your manservant or maidservant, nor your animals, nor the alien within your gates. For in six days the LORD made the heavens and the earth, the sea, and all that is in them, but he rested on the seventh day. Therefore the LORD blessed the Sabbath day and made it holy.

Honor your father and your mother, so that you may live long in the land the LORD your God is giving you.

You shall not murder.

You shall not commit adultery.

You shall not steal.

You shall not give false testimony against your neighbor.

You shall not covet your neighbor's house. You shall not covet your neighbor's wife, or his manservant or maidservant, his ox or donkey, or anything that belongs to your neighbor.

EXODUS 20:3-17

Our imitation of God in this life . . . must be an imitation of God incarnate; our model is the Jesus, not only of Calvary, but of the workshop, the roads, the crowds, the clamorous demands and surly oppositions, the lack of all peace and privacy, the interruptions. For this, so strangely unlike anything we can attribute to the Divine life in itself, is apparently not only like, but is, the Divine life operating under human conditions.

C. S. LEWIS

I have lived, sir, a long time, and the longer I live, the more convincing proofs I see of this truth—that God governs in the affairs of men. And if a sparrow cannot fall to the ground without His notice, is it probable that an empire can rise without His aid?

BENJAMIN FRANKLIN

We have been the recipients of the choicest bounties of heaven. We have been preserved, these many years, in peace and prosperity. We have grown in numbers, wealth, and power as no other nation has ever grown; but we have forgotten God. We have forgotten the gracious hand which preserved us in peace and multiplied and enriched and strengthened us; and we have vainly imagined, in the deceitfulness of our hearts, that all these blessings were produced by some superior wisdom and virtue of our own.

ABRAHAM LINCOLN

There is no greater drama in human record than the sight of a few Christians, scorned or oppressed by a succession of emperors, bearing all trials with a fierce tenacity, multiplying quietly, building order while their enemies generated chaos, fighting the sword with the word, brutality with hope, and at last defeating the strongest state that history has known. Caesar and Christ had met in the arena, and Christ had won.

WILL DURANT

Philosophical argument, especially that drawn from the vastness of the universe, in comparison with the apparent insignificance of this globe, has sometimes shaken my reason for the faith which is in me; but my heart has always assured me that the gospel of Jesus Christ must be divine reality. The Sermon on the Mount cannot be a mere human production. This belief enters into the very depth of my conscience. The whole history of man proves it.

DANIEL WEBSTER
(HIS EPITAPH, DICTATED THE DAY BEFORE HE DIED)

I have ever judged of the religion of others by their lives. It is in our lives, and not from our words, that our religion must be read. By the same test the world must judge me. But this does not satisfy the priesthood. They must have a positive, a declared assent to all their interested absurdities. My opinion is that there would never have been an infidel if there had never been a priest. The artificial structures they have built on the purest of all moral systems, for the purpose of deriving from it pence and power, revolt those who think for themselves, and who read in that system only what is really there.

THOMAS JEFFERSON

I have long believed there was a divine plan that placed this land here to be found by people of a special kind, that we have a rendezvous with destiny. Yes, there is a spirit moving in this land and a hunger in the people for a spiritual revival. If the task I seek should be given to me, I would pray only that I could perform it in a way that would serve God.

RONALD REAGAN

GOVERNMENT

Government is a trust, and the officers
of the government are trustees; and
both the trust and the trustees are
created for the benefit of the people.

HENRY CLAY

The government is the strongest of which every man
feels himself a part.

THOMAS JEFFERSON

It is the duty of government to make it difficult for
people to do wrong, easy to do right.

WILLIAM E. GLADSTONE

The best energies of my life have been spent in endeavoring to
establish and perpetuate the blessings of free government.

ANDREW JOHNSON

I go for all sharing the privileges of the government
who assist in bearing its burdens.

ABRAHAM LINCOLN

As the happiness of the people is the sole end of government,
so the consent of the people is the only foundation of it, in
reason, morality, and the natural fitness of things.

JOHN ADAMS

The will of the people is the only legitimate foundation of
any government, and to protect its free expression
should be our first object.

THOMAS JEFFERSON

A government is the only known vessel that
leaks from the top.

JAMES RESTON

It's getting harder and harder to support the government in
the style to which it has become accustomed.

FARMERS' ALMANAC

Men must be governed by God or they will be ruled by tyrants.

WILLIAM PENN

Government is like a baby—an alimentary canal with a big
appetite at one end and no sense of responsibility at the other.

RONALD REAGAN

I don't make jokes; I just watch the government and
report the facts.

WILL ROGERS

All Congresses and Parliaments have a kindly feeling
for idiots and a compassion for them, on
account of personal experience and heredity.

MARK TWAIN

Whenever you have an efficient government you
have a dictatorship.

HARRY S. TRUMAN

The nearest approach to immortality on earth is
a government bureau.

JAMES F. BYRNES

If we can prevent the government from wasting the labors of
the people, under the pretense of taking care of them, they
must become happy.

THOMAS JEFFERSON

My reading of history convinces me that most
bad government has grown out of too much government.

JOHN S. WILLIAMS

The marvel of all history is the patience with which
men and women submit to burdens unnecessarily laid upon
them by their governments.

WILLIAM E. BORAH

The office of government is not to confer happiness, but to
give men opportunity to work out happiness for themselves.

WILLIAM ELLERY CHANNING

For thirty years, the Bible-believing Christians of America
have been largely absent from the executive, legislative, and
judicial branches of both federal and local government.

JERRY FALWELL

Why has government been instituted at all?
Because the passions of men will not conform to the dictates
of reason and justice, without constraint.

ALEXANDER HAMILTON

The government is mainly an expensive organization
to regulate evildoers and tax those who behave; government
does little for fairly respectable people except annoy them.

EDGAR WATSON HOWE

A wise and frugal government, which shall restrain men from
injuring one another, shall leave them otherwise free to regulate
their own pursuits of industry and improvement, and shall not
take from the mouth of labor the bread it has earned. This is the
sum of good government, and this is necessary to close the circle
of our felicities.

THOMAS JEFFERSON

The legitimate object of government is to do for a community of people whatever they need to have done, but cannot do at all, or can't so well do for themselves in their separate and individual capacities. In all that the people can individually do as well for themselves, government ought not to interfere.

ABRAHAM LINCOLN

You must not complicate your government beyond the capacity of its electorate to understand it. If you do, it will escape all control, turn corrupt and tyrannical, lose the popular confidence, offer real security to no man, and in the end it will let loose all the submerged antagonisms within the state.

WALTER LIPPMANN

Government exists to protect rights which are ours from birth; the right to life, to liberty, and the pursuit of happiness. A man may choose to sit and fish instead of working—that's his pursuit of happiness. He does not have the right to force his neighbors to support him in his pursuit because that interferes with their pursuit of happiness.

RONALD REAGAN

Compromise makes a good umbrella, but a poor roof; it is a temporary expedient, often wise in party politics, almost sure to be unwise in statesmanship.

JAMES RUSSELL LOWELL

I only regret that I have but one life to lose for my country.

NATHAN HALE

Lord, the money we do spend on government and it's not one bit better than the government we got for one-third the money twenty years ago.

WILL ROGERS

THE GETTYSBURG ADDRESS

Fourscore and seven years ago our fathers brought forth upon this continent a new nation, conceived in liberty and dedicated to the proposition that all men are created equal.

Now we are engaged in a great civil war, testing whether that nation, or any nation so conceived and so dedicated, can long endure. We are met on a great battlefield of that war. We are met to dedicate a portion of it as the final resting place of those who here gave their lives that that nation might live. It is altogether fitting and proper that we should do this.

But in a larger sense we cannot dedicate, we cannot consecrate, we cannot hallow this ground. The brave men, living and dead, who struggled here, have consecrated it far above our poor power to add or detract. The world will little note, nor long remember, what we say here, but it can never forget what they did here. It is for us, the living, rather, to be dedicated here to the unfinished work that they have thus far so nobly carried on.

It is rather for us to be here dedicated to the great task remaining before us, that from these honored dead we take increased devotion to that cause for which they here gave the last full measure of devotion; that we here highly resolve that these dead shall not have died in vain; that the nation shall, under God, have a new birth of freedom; and that government of the people, by the people, for the people, shall not perish from the earth.

ABRAHAM LINCOLN

Too bad all the people who know how to run the country are
busy driving cabs and cutting hair.

GEORGE BURNS

Society in every state is a blessing, but government, even
in its best stage, is a necessary evil; in its worst state
an intolerable one.

THOMAS PAINE

Our average fellow-citizen is a sane and healthy man, who
believes in decency and has a wholesome mind.

THEODORE ROOSEVELT

The first requisite of a good citizen in this republic of ours is
that he shall be able and willing to pull his weight.

THEODORE ROOSEVELT

A citizen first in war, first in peace, and
first in the hearts of his countrymen.

HENRY LEE

The essence of government is power; and power, lodged as it
must be in human hands, will ever be liable to abuse.

JAMES MADISON

It may be laid down as a primary position, and the basis of our
system, that every citizen who enjoys the protection of a free
government, owes not only a proportion of his property, but
even his personal services to the defense of it, and consequently
that the citizens of America (with a few legal and official excep-
tions) from eighteen to fifty years of age should be borne on the
militia rolls, provided with uniform arms, and so far accustomed
to the use of them, that the total strength of the country might
be called forth at a short notice on any very interesting emergency.

GEORGE WASHINGTON

One of the virtues of a small-town politician is that he knows
he has to stick pretty close to the truth.

Any government, like any family, can for a year spend
a little more than it earns.
But you and I know that a continuation of
that habit means the poorhouse.

FRANKLIN D. ROOSEVELT

The ballot is stronger than the bullet.

ABRAHAM LINCOLN

None of us here in Washington knows all or even half of the
answers. You people out there in the fifty states had better
understand that. If you love your country, don't depend on
handouts from Washington for your information. If you cherish
your freedom, don't leave it all up to big government.

BARRY GOLDWATER

If the nation is living within its income, its credit is good. If in
some crisis it lives beyond its income for a year or two, it can
usually borrow temporarily on reasonable terms. But if, like the
spendthrift, it throws discretion to the winds, is willing to make
no sacrifice at all in spending, extends its taxing to the limit of
the people's power to pay, and continues to pile up deficits, it is
on the road to bankruptcy.

FRANKLIN D. ROOSEVELT

It does not require a lawyer to interpret the provisions of the
Bill of Rights. They are as clear as the Ten Commandments.

HERBERT HOOVER

The only thing that saves us from the bureaucracy is
its inefficiency.

EUGENE MCCARTHY

Will you please tell me what you do with all the vice presidents a bank has? I guess that's to get you more discouraged before you can see the president. Why, the United States is the biggest business institution in the world, and they only have one vice president and nobody has ever found anything for him to do.

WILL ROGERS

If we lose the virile, manly qualities, and sink into a nation of mere hucksters, putting gain over national honor, and subordinate everything to mere ease of life, then we shall indeed reach a condition worse than that of the ancient civilizations in the years of their decay.

THEODORE ROOSEVELT

On this showing, the nature of the breakdowns of civilizations can be summed up in three points: A failure of creative power in the minority, an answering withdrawal of mimesis on the part of the majority, and a consequent loss of social unity in the society as a whole.

ARNOLD J. TOYNBEE

Now civilizations, I believe, come to birth and proceed to grow by successfully responding to successive challenges. They break down and go to pieces if and when a challenge confronts them which they fail to meet.

ARNOLD J. TOYNBEE

The sum of the whole matter is this, that our civilization cannot survive materially unless it be redeemed spiritually.

WOODROW WILSON

What is a Communist?
One who has yearnings for equal division of unequal earnings.

EBENEZER ELLIOT

If the Communists worked just as hard as they talked, they'd have the most prosperous style of government in the world.

WILL ROGERS

They say that the Soviet delegates smile. That smile is genuine. It is not artificial. We wish to live in peace, tranquillity. But if anyone believes that our smiles involve abandonment of the teaching of Marx, Engels, and Lenin he deceives himself poorly. Those who wait for that must wait until a shrimp learns to whistle.

NIKITA S. KHRUSHCHEV

It is necessary to be able to withstand all this, to agree to any and every sacrifice, and even—if need be—to resort to all sorts of stratagems, maneuvers, and illegal methods, to evasion and subterfuges in order to penetrate the trade unions, to remain in them, and to carry on Communist work in them at all costs.

V. I. LENIN

Communist: One who has nothing and is
eager to share it with others.

It could probably be shown by facts and figures that
there is no distinctly native American criminal class
except Congress.

MARK TWAIN

With Congress, every time they make a joke it's a law, and
every time they make a law it's a joke.

WILL ROGERS

Reader, suppose you were an idiot.
And suppose you were a member of Congress.
But I repeat myself.

MARK TWAIN

I am now here in Congress. I am at liberty to vote as my conscience and judgment dictate to be right, without the yoke of any party on me, or the driver at my heels, with his whip in hand, commanding me to gee—whoa—haw, just at his pleasure.

DAVID CROCKETT

Congress is so strange. A man gets up to speak and says nothing. Nobody listens—and then everybody disagrees.

BORIS MARSHALOV

There are two periods when Congress does no business: one is before the holidays, and the other after.

GEORGE DENNISON PRENTICE

I have come to the conclusion that one useless man is called a disgrace, that two are called a law firm, and that three or more become a Congress.

PETER STONE

One of the standing jokes of Congress is that the new congressman always spends the first week wondering how he got there and the rest of the time wondering how the other members got there.

SATURDAY EVENING POST

This country has come to feel the same when Congress is in session as we do when the baby gets hold of a hammer. It's just a question of how much damage he can do with it before we can take it away from him.

WILL ROGERS

I venture to say that if you search the earth all over with a ten horsepower microscope, you won't be able to find such another pack of poppycock gabblers as the present Congress.

ARTEMUS WARD

You see, ordinarily you have got to work your way up
as a humorist, and first get into Congress.
Then you work your way up into the Senate and then, if
your stuff is funny enough, it goes into
the Congressional Record.

WILL ROGERS

Fleas can be taught nearly everything that a congressman can.

MARK TWAIN

You can't use tact with a congressman. A congressman is a
hog. You must take a stick and hit him on the snout.

HENRY ADAMS

To my mind Judas Iscariot was nothing but a low, mean,
premature congressman.

MARK TWAIN

If there be one principle more deeply rooted than
any other in the mind of every American, it is
that we should have nothing to do with conquest.

THOMAS JEFFERSON

The United States Constitution has proved itself the most
marvelous compilation of rules of government ever written.

FRANKLIN D. ROOSEVELT

To live under the American Constitution is the greatest
political privilege that was ever accorded to the human race.

CALVIN COOLIDGE

Don't interfere with anything in the Constitution.
That must be maintained, for it is the only
safeguard of our liberties.

ABRAHAM LINCOLN

It is too probable that no plan we propose will be adopted. Perhaps another dreadful conflict is to be sustained. If to please the people, we offer what we ourselves disapprove, how can we afterwards defend our work? Let us raise a standard to which the wise and the honest can repair. The event is in the hand of God.

GEORGE WASHINGTON

The Constitution of the United States was made not merely for the generation that then existed, but for posterity—unlimited, undefined, endless, perpetual posterity.

HENRY CLAY

As the British Constitution is the most subtle organism which has proceeded from progressive history, so the American Constitution is the most wonderful work ever struck off at a given time by the brain and purpose of man.

WILLIAM E. GLADSTONE

The Constitution . . . is unquestionably the wisest ever yet presented to men.

THOMAS JEFFERSON

Capital punishment: spending the summer in Washington, D. C.

And to preserve our independence, we must not let our rulers load us with perpetual debt. We must make our election between economy and liberty, or profusion and servitude.

THOMAS JEFFERSON

We must be willing, individually and as a nation, to accept whatever sacrifices may be required of us. A people that values its privileges above its principles soon loses both.

DWIGHT D. EISENHOWER

I am for a government rigorously frugal and simple, applying all the possible savings of the public revenue to the discharge of the national debt; and not for a multiplication of officers and salaries merely to make partisans, and for increasing, by every device, the public debt, on the principle of it's being a public blessing.

THOMAS JEFFERSON

I wish it were possible to obtain a single amendment to our Constitution. I would be willing to depend on that alone for the reduction of the administration of our government to the genuine principles of its Constitution; I mean an additional article, taking from the federal government the power of borrowing.

THOMAS JEFFERSON

The sum total of our national debt is some total.

I, however, place economy among the first and
most important of republican virtues, and public debt as
the greatest of the dangers to be feared.

THOMAS JEFFERSON

As an individual who undertakes to live by borrowing, soon
finds his original means devoured by interest, and
next no one left to borrow from—so
must it be with a government.

ABRAHAM LINCOLN

I sincerely believe . . . that banking establishments are more dangerous than standing armies, and that the principle of spending money to be paid by posterity, under the name of funding, is but swindling futurity on a large scale.

THOMAS JEFFERSON

Blessed are the young, for they shall inherit the national debt.

HERBERT HOOVER

A strong defense is the surest way to peace. Strength makes détente attainable. Weakness invites war, as my generation— my generation—knows from four very bitter experiences.

GERALD R. FORD

If we desire to avoid insult, we must be able to repel it; if we desire to secure peace, one of the most powerful instruments of our rising prosperity, it must be known that we are at all times ready for war.

GEORGE WASHINGTON

To be prepared for war is one of the most effectual means of preserving peace.

GEORGE WASHINGTON

The dogmas of the quiet past are inadequate to the stormy present. The occasion is piled high with difficulty, and we must rise with the occasion. As our case is new, so we must think anew and act anew.

ABRAHAM LINCOLN

Vote for the man who promises least; he'll be the least disappointing.

BERNARD M. BARUCH

I believe that biennial elections and quadrennial governorships are inventions which deprive the people of power, and at the same time offer prizes to be captured by the corruption of political life.

THOMAS BRACKETT REED

On the presidential coat of arms, the American eagle holds in his right talon an olive branch, while in his left he holds a bundle of arrows. We intend to give equal attention to both.

JOHN F. KENNEDY

The penalty good men pay for indifference to
public affairs is to be ruled by evil men.

PLATO

Hell hath no fury like a liberal scorned.

DICK GREGORY

I find honorary degrees always tempting, and
often bad for me: tempting because we all—even
ex-politicians—hope to be mistaken for scholars, and
bad because if you then make a speech
the mistake is quickly exposed.

ADLAI STEVENSON

Nothing appears more surprising to those
who consider human affairs with a philosophical eye, than
the ease with which the many are governed by the few.

DAVID HUME

Insurrection of thought always precedes insurrection of arms.

WENDELL PHILLIPS

One of the greatest delusions in the world is
the hope that the evils of this world can be cured by
legislation. I am happy in the belief
that the solution of the great difficulties of life and
government is in better hands even than those of this body.

THOMAS BRACKETT REED

No man's life, liberty, or property is safe while
the legislature is in session.

GIDEON J. TUCKER

Money is the principal export of the United States.

A rich man told me recently that a liberal is a man who tells
other people what to do with their money.

LEROI JONES

A liberal is a man who leaves the room when the fight begins.

HEYWOOD BROUN

A liberal is a man who is willing to spend
somebody else's money.

SENATOR CARTER GLASS

A liberal is a person whose interests aren't
at stake at the moment.

WILLIS PLAYER

A radical is a man with both feet firmly planted in the air.

FRANKLIN D. ROOSEVELT

Liberalism is the first refuge of political indifference and
the last refuge of leftists.

HARRY ROSKOLENKO

It is my principle that the will of the majority
should always prevail.

THOMAS JEFFERSON

Great nations rise and fall. The people go from bondage to spiritual truth, to great courage, from courage to liberty, from liberty
to abundance, from abundance to selfishness, from selfishness to
complacency, from complacency to apathy, from apathy to
dependence, from dependence back again to bondage.

BENJAMIN DISRAELI

I am not a member of any organized party—I am a Democrat.

WILL ROGERS

Having undertaken for the glory of God, and advancement of the Christian faith, and the honor of our king and country, a voyage to plant the first colony in the northern parts of Virginia; do by these presents, solemnly and mutually in the presence of God and one another, covenant and combine ourselves together into a civil body politic, for our better ordering and preservation, and furtherance of the ends aforesaid; and by virtue hereof to enact, constitute, and frame, such just and equal laws, ordinances, acts, constitutions and offices, from time to time, as shall be thought most meet and convenient for the general good of the colony; unto which we promise all due submission and obedience.

MAYFLOWER COMPACT

Persistence in one opinion has never been considered
a merit in political leaders.

CICERO

In a free and republican government, you cannot restrain the voice of the multitude. Every man will speak as he thinks or, more properly, without thinking, and consequently will judge of effects without attending to their causes.

GEORGE WASHINGTON

While the Republicans are smart enough to make money, the Democrats are smart enough to get in office every two or three times a century and take it away from 'em.

WILL ROGERS

Republicans study the financial pages of the newspaper.
Democrats put them in the bottom of the bird cage.

WILL STANTON

You've got to be [an] optimist to be a Democrat, and
you've got to be a humorist to stay one.

WILL ROGERS

Political parties serve to keep each other in check, one
keenly watching the other.

HENRY CLAY

I never said all Democrats were saloon-keepers.
What I said was that all saloon-keepers are Democrats.

HORACE GREELEY

What this country needs is more unemployed politicians.

EDWARD LANGLEY

He has been called a mediocre man, but this is unwarranted
flattery. He was a politician of monumental littleness.

THEODORE ROOSEVELT, WRITING OF JOHN TYLER

The politician is an acrobat; he keeps his balance by
saying the opposite of what he does.

MAURICE BARRES

[Politicians] are the same all over.
They promise to build a bridge even where there is no river.

NIKITA S. KHRUSHCHEV

I don't think it does any harm just once in a while to
acknowledge that the whole country isn't in flames, that
there are people in the country besides politicians,
entertainers, and criminals.

CHARLES KURALT

One thing our founding fathers could not foresee—they were
farmers, professional men, businessmen giving of their time and
effort to an idea that became a country—was a nation governed
by professional politicians who had a vested interest in getting
re-elected. They probably envisioned a fellow serving a couple
of hitches and then looking forward to getting back to the farm.

RONALD REAGAN

We do not elect our wisest and best men to represent us.
In general, we elect men of the type that subscribes to
only one principle—to get reelected.

TERRY M. TOWNSEND

An honest politician is one who when he is bought
will stay bought.

SIMON CAMERON

Since a politician never believes what he says, he
is surprised when others believe him.

CHARLES DE GAULLE

Walter Mondale has all the charisma of a speed bump.

WILL DURST

Mr. Lincoln is like a waiter in a large eating house where all
the bells are ringing at once; he cannot serve them all at once,
and so some grumblers are to be expected.

JOHN BRIGHT

Whenever a fellow tells me he's bipartisan, I know
he's going to vote against me.

HARRY S. TRUMAN

If experience teaches us anything at all, it teaches us
this: that a good politician, under democracy, is
quite as unthinkable as an honest burglar.

H. L. MENCKEN

Ninety-eight percent of the adults in this country are decent,
hard-working, honest Americans.
It's the other lousy two percent that get all the publicity.
But then—we elected them.

LILY TOMLIN

Man is by nature a political animal.

ARISTOTLE

Politics ought to be the part-time profession of every citizen who would protect the rights and privileges of free people and who would preserve what is good and fruitful in our national heritage.

DWIGHT D. EISENHOWER

In my youth, I, too, entertained some illusions; but I soon recovered from them. The great orators who rule the assemblies by the brilliancy of their eloquence are in general men of the most mediocre political talents; they should not be opposed in their own way, for they have always more noisy words at command than you. Their eloquence should be opposed by a serious and logical argument; their strength lies in vagueness; they should be brought back to the reality of facts; practical arguments destroy them. In the council, there were men possessed of much more eloquence than I was; I always defeated them by this simple argument—two and two makes four.

NAPOLEON

Practical politics consists in ignoring facts.

HENRY ADAMS

Politics is perhaps the only profession for which no preparation is thought necessary.

ROBERT LOUIS STEVENSON

Politics is such a torment that I would advise every one I love not to mix with it.

THOMAS JEFFERSON

The middle of the road is where the white line is—and that's the worst place to drive.

ROBERT FROST

Things get very lonely in Washington sometimes. The real voice of the great people of America sometimes sounds faint and distant in that strange city. You hear politics until you wish that both parties were smothered in their own gas.

WOODROW WILSON

The presidential campaign speech is, like jazz, one of the few truly American art forms. It is not, of course, unknown in other democratic countries, but nowhere else has it achieved the same degree of virtuosity; nowhere else is it so accurate a reflection of national character: by turns solemn or witty, pompous or deeply moving, full of sense or full of wind.

You heard the story, haven't you, about the man who was tarred and feathered and carried out of town on a rail? A man in the crowd asked him how he liked it. His reply was that if it was not for the honor of the thing, he would much rather walk.

ABRAHAM LINCOLN
(WHEN ASKED HOW HE LIKED BEING PRESIDENT)

I know well that no man will ever bring out of that office the reputation which carries him into it. The honeymoon would be as short in that case as in any other, and its moments of ecstasy would be ransomed by years of torment and hatred.

THOMAS JEFFERSON

With experience enough in subordinate offices to have seen the difficulties of this the greatest of all, I have learned to expect that it will rarely fall to the lot of imperfect man to retire from this station with the reputation and the favor which bring him into it.

THOMAS JEFFERSON

No president who performs his duties faithfully and conscientiously can have any leisure.

JAMES K. POLK

A great civilization is not conquered from without until it has destroyed itself within. The essential causes of Rome's decline lay in her people, her morals, her class struggle, her failing trade, her bureaucratic despotism, her stifling taxes, her consuming wars.

WILL DURANT

Every revolution was first a thought in one man's mind.

RALPH WALDO EMERSON

No man is good enough to govern another man without that other's consent.

ABRAHAM LINCOLN

A man must first care for his own household before he can be of use to the state. But no matter how well he cares for his household, he is not a good citizen unless he also takes thought of the state. In the same way, a great nation must think of its own internal affairs; and yet it cannot substantiate its claim to be a great nation unless it also thinks of its position in the world at large.

THEODORE ROOSEVELT

Any people anywhere, being inclined and having the power, have the right to rise up and shake off the existing government and form a new one that suits them better. This is a most valuable, a most sacred right, a right which we hope and believe is to liberate the world. Nor is this right confined to cases in which the whole people of an existing government may choose to exercise it. Any portion of such people that can, may revolutionize and make their own of so much of the territory as they inhabit. More than this, a majority of any portion of such people may revolutionize, putting down a minority, intermingled with, or near about them, who may oppose their movement.

ABRAHAM LINCOLN

I say the right of a state to annul a law of Congress cannot be maintained but on the ground of the inalienable right of man to resist oppression; that is to say, upon the ground of revolution.

DANIEL WEBSTER

This country, with its institutions, belongs to the people who inhabit it. Whenever they shall grow weary of the existing government, they can exercise their constitutional right of amending it or their revolutionary right to dismember or overthrow it.

ABRAHAM LINCOLN

The U. S. Senate may not be the most refined and deliberative body in existence, but they've got the most unique rules. Any member can call anybody in the world anything he can think of and they can't answer him, sue him, or fight him. Our Constitution protects aliens, drunks, and U. S. senators. There ought to be one day (just one) where there is an open season on senators.

WILL ROGERS

I believe if we introduced the Lord's Prayer here, senators would propose a large number of amendments to it.
I believe each individual is naturally entitled to do as he pleases with himself and the fruit of his labor, so far as it in no wise interferes with any other man's rights—that each community, as a state, has a right to do exactly as it pleases with all concerns within that state that interfere with the right of no other state, and that the general government, upon principle, has no right to interfere with anything other than that general class of things that does concern the whole.

ABRAHAM LINCOLN

The states should be left to do whatever acts they can do as well as the general government.

THOMAS JEFFERSON

Asking one of the states to surrender part of her sovereignty is like asking a lady to surrender part of her chastity.

JOHN RANDOLPH

The maintenance inviolate of the rights of the states, and especially the right of each state to order and control its own domestic institutions according to its own judgment exclusively, is essential to that balance of powers on which the perfection and endurance of our political fabric depends.

ABRAHAM LINCOLN

What an augmentation of the field for jobbing, speculating, plundering, office-building, and office-hunting would be produced by an assumption of all the state powers into the hand of the general government! The true theory of our Constitution is surely the wisest and best, that the states are independent as to everything within themselves and united as to everything respecting foreign nations. Let the general government be reduced to foreign concerns only.

THOMAS JEFFERSON

The first requirement of a statesman is that he be dull. This is not always easy to achieve.

DEAN ACHESON

You can always get the truth from an American statesman after he has turned seventy, or given up all hope of the presidency.

WENDELL PHILLIPS

I have sworn upon the altar of God, eternal hostility against every form of tyranny over the mind of man.

THOMAS JEFFERSON

A society of sheep must in time beget a government of wolves.

DE JOUVENAL

When a people shall have become incapable of governing
themselves, and fit for a master, it is of little consequence
from what quarter he comes.

GEORGE WASHINGTON

I'm sure everyone feels sorry for the individual who has fallen by
the wayside or who can't keep up in our competitive society, but
my own compassion goes beyond that to those millions of
unsung men and women who get up every morning, send the
kids to school, go to work, try to keep up the payments on their
house, pay exorbitant taxes to make possible compassion for the
less fortunate, and as a result have to sacrifice many of their own
desires and dreams and hopes. Government owes them something better than always finding a new way to make them share
the fruit of their toils with others.

RONALD REAGAN

Once there were two brothers.
One ran away to sea, the other was elected vice president,
and nothing was ever heard of them again.

THOMAS MARSHALL

The vice presidency is sort of like the last cookie on the plate.
Everybody insists he won't take it, but somebody always does.

BILL VAUGHAN

The vice president is like a man in a cataleptic state: he
cannot speak, he cannot move, he suffers no pain, and
yet he is perfectly conscious of everything
that is going on around him.

THOMAS R. MARSHALL

My country has in its wisdom contrived for me the most
insignificant office that ever the invention of man contrived
or his imagination conceived.

JOHN ADAMS

Perhaps the best way to get people out to vote would be to
propose a law which wouldn't let them.

The right of voting for representatives is
the primary right by which other rights are protected.
To take away this right is to reduce a man to slavery, for
slavery consists in being subject to the will of another, and he
that has not a vote in the election of representatives
is in this case.

THOMAS PAINE

Knowledge of human nature is the beginning and
end of political education.

HENRY ADAMS

If forced to choose between the penitentiary and
the White House for four years . . .
I would say the penitentiary, thank you.

WILLIAM T. SHERMAN

This absorption of revenue by all levels of government, the
alarming rate of inflation, and the rising toll of unemployment
all stem from a single source: the belief that government, particularly the federal government, has the answer to our ills, and
that the proper method of dealing with social problems is to
transfer power from the private to the public sector, and within
the public sector from state and local governments to the ulti-
mate power center in Washington. This collectivist, centralizing
approach, whatever name or party label it wears, has created our
economic problems.

RONALD REAGAN

I think our governments will remain virtuous for many centuries; as long as they are chiefly agricultural; and this will be as long as there shall be vacant lands in any part of America. When they get piled upon one another in large cities, as in Europe, they will become corrupt as in Europe.

THOMAS JEFFERSON

HAPPINESS

Happiness is a perfume you cannot
pour on others without getting a few
drops on yourself.

GEORGE BERNARD SHAW

We act as though comfort and luxury
were the chief requirements of life, when
all that we need to make us really happy is
something to be enthusiastic about.

CHARLES KINGSLEY

The door to happiness opens outwards.

SOREN KIERKEGAARD

Happiness consists in being happy with
what we have got and with what we haven't got.

CHARLES H. SPURGEON

Success is getting what you want.
Happiness is wanting what you get.

Happiness is the natural flower of duty.

PHILLIPS BROOKS

It's pretty hard to tell what does bring happiness.
Poverty an' wealth have both failed.

FRANK MCKINNEY HUBBARD

Grief can take care of itself; but to get the full value
of a joy you must have somebody to divide it with.

MARK TWAIN

All you need for happiness is a good gun, a
good horse, and a good wife.

DANIEL BOONE

I had rather be shut up in a very modest cottage, with my books,
my family, and a few old friends, dining on simple bacon, and
letting the world roll on as it liked, than to occupy the most
splendid post which any human power can give.

THOMAS JEFFERSON

Happiness in this world, when it comes, comes incidentally.
Make it the object of pursuit, and it leads us on a wild-goose
chase, and is never attained. Follow some other object, and very
possibly we may find that we have caught happiness without
dreaming of it.

NATHANIEL HAWTHORNE

There are eight requisites for contented living: health enough
to make work a pleasure; wealth enough to support your needs;
strength enough to battle with difficulties and overcome them;
patience enough to toil until some good is accomplished; charity
enough to see some good in your neighbor; love enough to
move you to be useful and helpful to others; faith enough to
make real the things of God; hope enough to remove all anxious fears concerning the future.

GOETHE

There's an Oriental story about two friends who stood on a
bridge watching the fish in a stream below. "How happy the
fishes are," observed one. "You're not a fish," said his friend.
"How can you know whether they're happy or not?" "You're not
me," the first man replied. "How can you know whether I know
whether fish are happy or not?"

EDWIN WAY TEALE

A happy heart is better than a full purse.

A happy heart makes the face cheerful, but
heartache crushes the spirit.

PROVERBS 15:13

That everyone may eat and drink, and find satisfaction
in all his toil—this is the gift of God.

ECCLESIASTES 3:13

The best way to secure future happiness is to be as happy
as is rightfully possible today.

CHARLES W. ELIOTT

A truly happy person is one who can smile from year to year.

One of the first lessons to learn in life is that you can make
some people deliriously happy simply by letting them alone.

We can find something enjoyable in any situation, no matter
how disagreeable, if we look for it.

Moderation is the key of lasting enjoyment.

Happiness is homemade.

The really happy man is the one who can enjoy
the scenery when he has to take a detour.

The surest way to lose the best in life is to fail to
recognize it when you already have it.

The best way to cheer yourself up is to
try to cheer someone else up.

MARK TWAIN

Lord, when I am tempted to complain, remind me
that I have been given far more than I have given.

He that's content hath enough;
He that complains, has too much.

BENJAMIN FRANKLIN

The only time an indelible memory is an advantage is when it
works best at remembering your blessings.

The surest way to be miserable is to have the leisure
to wonder whether or not you are happy.

GEORGE BERNARD SHAW

Follow pleasure, and then will pleasure flee.
Flee pleasure, and pleasure will follow thee.

JOHN HEYWOOD

He is richest who is content with the least, for
content is the wealth of nature.

SOCRATES

Ultimately the bond of all companionship, whether
in marriage or in friendship, is conversation.

OSCAR WILDE

HONESTY

I hope I shall always possess firmness
and virtue enough to maintain what
I consider the most enviable of all
titles, the character of an "honest man."

GEORGE WASHINGTON

Aggressive fighting for the right is the noblest sport
the world affords.

THEODORE ROOSEVELT

Nothing is politically right which is morally wrong.

DANIEL O'CONNELL

I have no idea what the mind
of a low-life scoundrel is like, but I know what
the mind of anhonest man is like:
It is terrifying.

ABEL HERMANT

There's one way to find out if a man is honest—ask him.
If he says "yes," you know he is crooked.

GROUCHO MARX

A yawn is at least an honest opinion.

A man can build a staunch reputation for honesty by
admitting he was in error, especially
when he gets caught at it.

ROBERT RUARK

Honesty in a person means nothing until he is tested
under circumstances when he is sure he could
get away with dishonesty.

Some persons who preach that honesty is the best policy
give you the impression that they haven't paid
a premium in a long time.

Labor to keep alive in your breast that little spark
of celestial fire—conscience.

GEORGE WASHINGTON

A good conscience is a continual Christmas.

BENJAMIN FRANKLIN

Conscience is the inner voice that warns us
that someone may be looking.

H. L. MENCKEN

I have noticed my conscience for many years, and
I know it is more trouble and bother to me than
anything else I started with.

MARK TWAIN

A clear conscience is a good pillow.

A clear conscience sleeps during thunder.

A good conscience is a continual feast.

A quiet conscience causes a quiet sleep.

Conscience is what makes a boy tell his mother
before his sister does.

Removing a man's conscience is usually
just a minor operation.

JESSE S. JONES

KINDNESS

Kindness in words creates confidence;
kindness in thinking creates profoundness;
kindness in giving creates love.

LAO-TSE

A kind man benefits himself, but
a cruel man brings trouble on himself.

PROVERBS 11:17

Pleasant words are a honeycomb, sweet
to the soul and healing to the bones.

PROVERBS 16:24

Treat people as if they were what they ought to be and you
help them to become what they are capable of being.

GOETHE

Shall we make a new rule of life from tonight: always
to try to be a little kinder than is necessary.

JAMES M. BARRIE

It is never too soon to do a kindness, for
one does not know how soon it will be too late.

FRIENDLY CHATS

Constant kindness can accomplish much.
As the sun makes ice melt, kindness
causes misunderstanding, mistrust
and hostility to evaporate.

ALBERT SCHWEITZER

I would like to have engraved inside
every wedding band: "Be kind to one another."
This is the golden rule of marriage, and the secret of
making love last through the years.

RANDOLPH RAY

Kind words can be short and easy to speak, but their echoes
are truly endless.

MOTHER TERESA

Kindness is Christianity with its work clothes on.

Kindness and evil are not forgotten.

We're not primarily put on this earth to see through
one another, but to see one another through.

PETER DE VRIES

A candle loses nothing of its light by lighting another candle.

Feel for others—in your pocket.

CHARLES H. SPURGEON

Charity is also a habit.

Don't be a noble fighter, 'cause kindness is righter.

POPEYE

Compassion will cure more sins than condemnation.

HENRY WARD BEECHER

If we could read the secret history of our enemies, we
should find in each man's life sorrow and suffering
enough to disarm all hostilities.

HENRY W. LONGFELLOW

What you keep is lost—what you give is forever yours.

SHOTA RUSTAVELI

In this world, it is not what we take up, but what we give up,
that makes us rich.

HENRY WARD BEECHER

Anxious hearts are very heavy, but
a word of encouragement does wonders.

He who gives while he lives
Also knows where it goes.

PERCY ROSS

In giving till it hurts, some people are extremely
sensitive to pain.

Nothing makes one feel so strong as a call for help.

GEORGE MACDONALD

There is one pleasure that the human being cannot tire of,
and that is the pleasure that comes from helping
someone who really needs you.

It is easy to help him who is willing to be helped.

A willing helper does not wait until he is asked.

Joy is one of the few things that is multiplied
when it is divided.

Pity and forbearance should characterize all acts of justice.

BENJAMIN FRANKLIN

Lending should be done with witnesses; giving,
without witnesses.

One man gives freely, yet gains even more; another
withholds unduly, but comes to poverty. A generous man will
prosper; he who refreshes others will himself be refreshed.

PROVERBS 11:24-25

Those who bring sunshine to the lives of others
cannot keep it from themselves.

JAMES M. BARRIE

Blessed are those who can give without remembering, and
take without forgetting.

ELIZABETH BIBESCO

Trust men, and they will be true to you; treat them greatly,
and they will show themselves great.

RALPH WALDO EMERSON

He that does good to another does good also to himself, not
only in the consequence, but in the very act.
For the consciousness of well-doing is in itself ample reward.

SENECA

The deepest principle in human nature is
the craving to be appreciated.

WILLIAM JAMES

The greatest pleasure I know is to do a good action by stealth,
and to have it found out by accident.

CHARLES LAMB

Let the giver be silent and the receiver speak.

One can endure sorrow alone, but it takes two to be glad.

ELBERT HUBBARD

LAUGHTER

The world is a looking glass and
gives back to every man the reflection
of his own face. Frown at it, and it
will in turn look sourly upon you;
laugh at it, and with it, and it is
a jolly kind companion.

WILLIAM M. THACKERAY

The fact is I have always believed that a good laugh was
good for both the mental and the physical digestion.

ABRAHAM LINCOLN

I laugh because I must not weep—that's all, that's all.

ABRAHAM LINCOLN

Mirth is God's medicine.

HENRY WARD BEECHER

Strange, when you come to think of it, that
of all the countless folk who have lived before our time
on this planet not one is known in history or
in legend as having died of laughter.

MAX BEERBOHM

Laughter is the sensation of feeling good all over, and
showing it principally in one spot.

JOSH BILLINGS

No one is more profoundly sad than he who laughs too much.

JEAN PAUL RICHTER

It is a great art to laugh at your own misfortunes.

Laughter is not a bad beginning for a friendship, and
it is the best ending for one.

OSCAR WILDE

Laughter and tears are meant to turn the wheels of the same
machinery of sensibility; one is a wind-power and the other
water-power, that is all.

OLIVER WENDELL HOLMES

The most completely lost of all days is the one
in which I have not laughed.

Accordion, n. An instrument in harmony with
the sentiments of an assassin.

AMBROSE BIERCE

Guess the serpent in the Garden of Eden was a garter snake.

REFLECTIONS OF A BACHELOR

Adam's rib: the original bone of contention.

OLIVER HERFORD, JOHN CLAY

The years between fifty and seventy are the hardest.
You are always being asked to do things, and yet
you are not decrepit enough to turn them down.

T. S. ELIOT

One of the most satisfying sights during air travel is
the one when you arrive at the baggage-claim location
and spot your luggage.

The animals are not as stupid as one thinks—they
have neither doctors nor lawyers.

L. DOCQUIER

The baby wakes up in the wee wee hours of the morning.

ROBERT ROBBINS

Animals have these advantages over man: They have
no theologians to instruct them, their funerals cost them
nothing, and no one starts lawsuits over their wills.

VOLTAIRE

Twenty-four years ago, madam, I was incredibly handsome.
The remains of it are still visible through the rift of time.
I was so handsome that women became spellbound when I
came in view. In San Francisco, in rainy seasons, I
was frequently mistaken for a cloudless day.

MARK TWAIN

There is something about a home aquarium which sets
my teeth on edge the moment I see it.
Why anyone should want to live with a small container of
stagnant water populated by a half-dead guppy is beyond me.

S. J. PERELMAN

The physician can bury his mistakes, but the architect
can only advise his clients to plant vines.

FRANK LLOYD WRIGHT

Very few people possess true artistic ability.
It is therefore both unseemly and unproductive to
irritate the situation by making an effort.
If you have a burning, restless urge to write or paint, simply
eat something sweet and the feeling will pass.

FRAN LEBOWITZ

There ain't nothing that breaks up homes, country, and
nations like somebody publishing their memoirs.

WILL ROGERS

The ideal woman . . . the dream of a man who
will be a bachelor all his life.

W. BURTON BALDRY

Bachelors know more about women than married men.
If they didn't, they'd be married too.

H. L. MENCKEN

A man laughs at a woman who puts on eyebrow makeup, but
spends ten minutes trying to comb two hairs
across a bald spot.

Bachelor: a man who never makes the same mistake once.

ED WYNN

The average girl would rather have beauty than brains,
because she knows that the average man can see
much better than he can think.

I'm tired of all this nonsense about beauty being only
skin-deep. That's deep enough.
What do you want—an adorable pancreas?

JEAN KERR

When I go to the beauty parlor, I always use the emergency
entrance. Sometimes I just go for an estimate.

PHYLLIS DILLER

A considerate doctor is one who never mails his bills
until he's sure the patients are well enough to receive them.

When I was born, I was so surprised I couldn't talk
for a year and a half.

GRACIE ALLEN

The blunders of physicians are covered by the earth.

From the moment I picked it [a book] up until
I laid it down, I was convulsed with laughter.
Someday I intend reading it.

GROUCHO MARX

This is not a novel to be tossed aside lightly.
It should be thrown with great force.

DOROTHY PARKER

A bore is a man who, when you ask him how he is, tells you.

BERT LESTON TAYLOR

He's the kind of bore who's here today and here tomorrow.

BINNIE BARNES

Men who say they are the boss in their own home
will lie about other things, too.

Some fellers' idea o' being funny is breakin' a few bones
when they shake your hand.

FRANK MCKINNEY HUBBARD

I have just returned from Boston.
It is the only thing to do if you find yourself up there.

FRED ALLEN

A committee is a group that keeps minutes and loses hours.

MILTON BERLE

It's a scientific fact that if you stay in California, you
lose one point of IQ every year.

TRUMAN CAPOTE

I came across a tribe of cannibals who'd been converted by
Roman Catholic missionaries.
Now, on Friday, they only eat fishermen.

MAX KAUFFMANN

Cats are intended to teach us that not everything
in nature has a purpose.

GARRISON KEILLOR

We've got a cat called Ben Hur.
We called it Ben till it had kittens.

SALLY POPLIN

A good loser is a person who can stick to a diet.

Poets have been mysteriously silent on the subject of cheese.

G. K. CHESTERTON

His books are selling like wildfire. Everybody's burning them.

GEORGE DEWITT

Have I got a mother-in-law.
She's so neat she puts paper under the cuckoo clock.

HENNY YOUNGMAN

We cannot put the face of a person on a stamp unless
said person is deceased.
My suggestion, therefore, is that you drop dead.

JAMES EDWARD DAY

Banker: a fellow who lends you his umbrella
when the sun is shining and wants it back
the minute it begins to rain.

MARK TWAIN

Why can't somebody give us a list of things everybody thinks
and nobody says, and another list of things that
everybody says and nobody thinks?

OLIVER WENDELL HOLMES

Here's to our town—a place where people spend money
they haven't earned to buy things they don't need
to impress people they don't like.

LEWIS C. HENRY

Money doesn't burn holes in pockets anymore—it
doesn't stay around long enough to even warm the lining.

The advantage of doing one's praising for oneself is that one
can lay it on so thick and exactly in the right places.

SAMUEL BUTLER

Don't tell me that worry doesn't do any good.
The things I worry about don't happen!

Life's too short for chess.

HENRY JAMES BYRON

When it comes to Chinese food . . . the less known
about the preparation the better.

CALVIN TRILLIN

Chop, n. A piece of leather skillfully attached to a bone and
administered to the patients at restaurants.

AMBROSE BIERCE

He charged nothing for his preaching, and
it was worth it, too.

MARK TWAIN

The last place people want to hang clothes is
their clothes closet. Closets are mean, inconvenient, often
dark and always overcrowded. If a person's closet isn't
overcrowded, you can bet that person needs a psychiatrist.

ANDY ROONEY

I hate being placed on committees. They are always
having meetings at which half are absent and the rest late.

OLIVER WENDELL HOLMES

There is so little difference between husbands, you
might as well keep the first.

ADELA ROGERS

Many are called. But few are called back.

SISTER MARY TRICKY

To err is human, but to really foul things up
requires a computer.

Dear Ned,
    Soon after I received my Acme pencil (11 cents), it rolled
off the desk and onto the floor. Upon retrieving it, I hit my head
on the desk. Can I hold Acme responsible?

BOILING MAD

The trouble with telling a good story is that it invariably
reminds the other fellow of a bad one.

SID CAESAR

Repartee is what you think of on the way home.

A gossip is one who talks to you about others, a bore
is one who talks to you about himself, and a brilliant
conversationalist is one who talks to you about yourself.

LISA KIRK

Corporation, n. An ingenious device for obtaining
individual profit without individual responsibility.

AMBROSE BIERCE

The cost of living is always about the same—all a person has.

In a courtship the heart beats so loudly it blocks out
the sound from the mind.

BERN WILLIAMS

There cannot be a crisis next week. My schedule is already full.

HENRY KISSINGER

Why can't our neighbors do as we do, and
close their eyes to our faults?

You can fool too many of the people too much of the time.

JAMES THURBER

A cucumber should be well sliced and dressed with pepper and
vinegar, and then thrown out, as good for nothing.

SAMUEL JOHNSON

Custard, n. A detestable substance produced
by a malevolent conspiracy of the hen,
the cow, and the cook.

AMBROSE BIERCE

Darling: the popular form of address used in speaking to
a member of the opposite sex whose name you
cannot at the moment remember.

OLIVER HERFORD

For three days after death, hair and fingernails continue to
grow but phone calls taper off.

JOHNNY CARSON

Running into debt isn't so bad.
It's running into creditors that hurts.

JACOB M. BRAUDE

Some problems are so complex that you have to be
highly intelligent and well-informed
just to be undecided about them.

LAURENCE J. PETER

He's turned his life around. He used to be depressed and
miserable. Now he's miserable and depressed.

DAVID FROST

Diplomats are just as essential to starting a war as
soldiers are for finishing it.

WILL ROGERS

No diet will remove all the fat from your body
because the brain is entirely fat. Without a brain you
might look good, but all you could do is run for public office.

COVERT BAILEY

You take diplomacy out of war and the thing would
fall flat in a week.

WILL ROGERS

Divorce is so common that some couples stay married
just to be different.

It is a good idea to "shop around" before you settle on
a doctor. Ask about the condition of his Mercedes.
Ask about the competence of his mechanic.
Don't be shy! After all, you're paying for it.

DAVE BARRY

We may lay it down as a maxim, that when a nation abounds
in physicians it grows thin of people.

JOSEPH ADDISON

I die by the help of too many physicians.

ALEXANDER THE GREAT

When in doubt, mumble; when in trouble,
delegate; when in charge, ponder.

JAMES H. BOREN

Doctors are just the same as lawyers; the only difference is
that lawyers merely rob you, whereas doctors rob you
and kill you, too.

ANTON CHEKHOV

My doctor is so busy, while in his waiting room
I caught another disease.

A dog teaches a body fidelity, perseverance, and
to turn 'round three times before lying down.

ROBERT BENCHLEY

A dog is the only thing on earth that loves
you more than you love yourself.

JOSH BILLINGS

If a dog could talk, he wouldn't be
man's best friend for long.

A careful driver is one who is following a traffic cop.

Early morning cheerfulness can be extremely obnoxious.

WILLIAM FEATHER

The horror of getting up is unparalleled, and I am filled with amazement every morning when I find that I have done it.

LYTTON STRACHEY

The only time my son washes his ears is when he eats watermelon.

Part of the secret of success in life is to eat what you like and let the food fight it out inside.

MARK TWAIN

For years I ate with the wrong fingers.
It's a sure sign somebody has been thinking about you when you find a tack in your chair.

Nothing improves the use of a young girl's left hand like a new engagement ring on it.

I'm astounded by people who want to "know" the universe when it's hard enough to find your way around Chinatown.

WOODY ALLEN

All men are born equal, but quite a few eventually get over it.

LORD MANCROFT

Etiquette is yawning with your mouth closed.

All modern men are descended from worm-like creatures, but it shows more on some people.

WILL CUPPY

I like long walks, especially when they are taken by people who annoy me.

FRED ALLEN

It's easy for most of us to meet expenses—we meet them everywhere we turn.

A celebrity is a person who works hard all his life to
become well known, and then wears dark glasses to
avoid being recognized.

FRED ALLEN

Everything you read in the newspaper is absolutely true,
except for that rare story of which you happen
to have firsthand knowledge.

ERWIN KNOLL

High heels: invented by a woman who had been
kissed on the forehead.

CHRISTOPHER MORLEY

Great is bankruptcy: the great bottomless gulf into which all
falsehoods, public and private, do sink, disappearing.

THOMAS CARLYLE

Failure has gone to his head.

WILSON MIZNER

In Mexico we have a word for sushi: bait.

JOSE SIMON

Never eat more than you can lift.

MISS PIGGY

The last time I had a hot meal was when
a candle fell in my TV dinner.

I broke our dog from begging for food from the table.
I let him taste it.

How can you be expected to govern a country that has two
hundred and forty-six kinds of cheese?

CHARLES DE GAULLE

France has neither winter nor summer nor morals—apart from these drawbacks it is a fine country.

MARK TWAIN

If you get gloomy, just take an hour off and sit and think how much better this world is than hell. Of course, it won't cheer you up if you expect to go there.

DON MARQUIS

The man and woman who can laugh at their love, who can kiss with smiles and embrace with chuckles, will outlast in mutual affection all the throat-lumpy, cow-eyed couples of their acquaintance. Nothing lives on so fresh and evergreen as the love with a funny bone.

If your garage is too small, you can always enlarge it by having your wife park your car.

Nothing is more responsible for the good old days than a bad memory.

FRANKLIN P. ADAMS

Gardening is man's effort to improve his lot.

I had great luck with my garden this year—nothing came up.

The good old days! I won't say I'm out of condition now—but I even puff going downstairs.

DICK GREGORY

To be good is noble, but to teach others how to be good is nobler—and less trouble.

MARK TWAIN

Quit worrying about your health. It'll go away.

ROBERT ORBEN

The only way to keep your health is to eat what you don't want, drink what you don't like, and do what you'd rather not. The average heart specialist can usually check the condition of his patient's heart simply by sending him a bill.

MARK TWAIN

I'd horsewhip you if I had a horse.

GROUCHO MARX

There have been many definitions of hell, but for the English the best definition is that it is a place where the Germans are the police, the Swedish are the comedians, the Italians are the defense force, Frenchmen dig the roads, the Belgians are the pop singers, the Spanish run the railways, the Turks cook the food, the Irish are the waiters, the Greeks run the government, and the common language is Dutch.

DAVID FROST

Very few things happen at the right time, and the rest do not happen at all. The conscientious historian will correct these defects.

HERODOTUS

Holidays are often overrated disturbances of routine, costly and uncomfortable; and they usually need another holiday to correct their ravages.

EDWARD VERRALL LUCAS

You can take all the sincerity in Hollywood, place it in the navel of a fruit fly, and still have room enough for three caraway seeds and a producer's heart.

FRED ALLEN

Hollywood is a city in the U. S. where someone is more likely to ask you Who's Whose than Who's Who.

When you've killed the sense of humor of a nation, you've
killed the nation.

RED SKELTON

The absolute truth is the thing that makes people laugh.

CARL REINER

One doesn't have a sense of humor.
It has you.

LARRY GELBART

You can teach taste and editorial sense, but
the ability to say something funny is something I've
never been able to teach anyone.

ABE BURROWS

Lord, give me a sense of humor that I may take
some happiness from this life and share it with others.

THOMAS MOORE

A little levity will save many a good heavy thing
from sinking.

SAMUEL BUTLER

Men will confess to treason, murder, arson, false teeth, or
a wig. How many of them will own up to a lack of humor?

FRANK MOORE COLBY

If Adam came on earth again, the only thing he
would recognize would be the old jokes.

THOMAS ROBERT DEWAR

Humor is when the joke is on you but
hits the other fellow first—before it boomerangs.

LANGSTON HUGHES

A pun is the lowest form of humor—when
you don't think of it first.

OSCAR LEVANT

Think of what would happen to us in America if there were
no humorists; life would be one long Congressional Record.

THOMAS L. MASSON

If ignorance is bliss, why aren't there more happy people?
Of puns it has been said that they who most dislike them
are least able to utter them.

EDGAR ALLAN POE

For every ten jokes, thou hast got an hundred enemies.

LAURENCE STERNE

Mark my words, when a society has to resort to the lavatory
for its humor, the writing is on the wall.

ALAN BENNETT

Gross ignorance—144 times worse than ordinary ignorance.

BENNETT CERF

He was distinguished for ignorance, for
he had only one idea and that was wrong.

BENJAMIN DISRAELI

Even his ignorance is encyclopedic.

STANISLAW J. LEC

What he doesn't know would make a library
anybody would be proud of.

Income tax returns are the most imaginative fiction
being written today.

His indecision is final.

Among the things that money can't buy is what it used to.

MAX KAUFFMANN

Invest in inflation. It's the only thing going up.

WILL ROGERS

Inflation has created a new economic problem: windfall poverty.
What passes for woman's intuition is often nothing more than
man's transparency.

GEORGE JEAN NATHAN

Today a dollar saved is a quarter earned.

Anyone can become wealthy in America by inventing
something useful that doesn't last long—like
most home appliances.

Never keep up with the Joneses.
Drag them down to your level; it's cheaper.

QUENTIN CRISP

The jury system puts a ban upon intelligence and honesty, and
a premium upon ignorance, stupidity, and perjury.

MARK TWAIN

We have a criminal jury system which is superior to any in the
world; and its efficiency is only marred by the difficulty of finding
twelve men every day who don't know anything and can't read.

MARK TWAIN

Everyone's talking about how young the candidates are. And it's
true. A few months ago Kennedy's mother said, "You have a choice
. . . do you want to go to camp this year or run for president?"

BOB HOPE

Personally I don't think you can make a lawyer honest by an act of legislature. You've got to work on his conscience. And his lack of conscience is what makes him a lawyer.

WILL ROGERS

I am not young enough to know everything.

JAMES M. BARRIE

I was told by a person who said that he was studying for the ministry that even Noah got no salary for the first six months—partly on account of the weather and partly because he was learning navigation.

MARK TWAIN

I've been on a calendar, but never on time.

MARILYN MONROE

A lawyer is a learned gentleman who rescues your estate from your enemies and keeps it for himself.

LORD BROUGHAM

Lawyer: one who protects us against robbers by taking away the temptation.

H. L. MENCKEN

The first thing we do, let's kill all the lawyers.

WILLIAM SHAKESPEARE

Ignorance of the law does not prevent the losing lawyer from collecting his bill.

PUCK

Never blame a legislative body for not doing something. When they do nothing, that don't hurt anybody. When they do something is when they become dangerous.

WILL ROGERS

One of the pleasures of reading old letters is the knowledge that they need no answer.

LORD BYRON

A classic is something that everybody wants to have read and nobody wants to read.

MARK TWAIN

A work of art? It has no invention; it has no order, system, sequence, or result; it has no lifelikeness, no thrill, no stir, no seeming of reality; its characters are confusedly drawn, and by their acts and words they prove that they are not the sort of people the author claims that they are; its humor is pathetic; its pathos is funny; its conversations are—oh! indescribable; its love scenes odious, its English a crime against the language. Counting these out, what is left is art. I think we must all admit that.

MARK TWAIN

If most auto accidents happen within five miles of home, why don't we move ten miles away?

MICHAEL DAVIS

The difference between Los Angeles and yogurt is that yogurt has an active, living culture.

I suppose it is much more comfortable to be mad and not know it, than to be sane and have one's doubts.

G. B. BURGIN

Want some fun? Send a get-well card to a hypochondriac.

Good breeding consists in concealing how much we think of ourselves and how little we think of the other person.

MARK TWAIN

Mathematics: a wonderful science, but it hasn't yet come up with a way to divide one tricycle between three small boys.

EARL WILSON

I was always taught to respect my elders, and I've now reached the age when I don't have anybody to respect.

GEORGE BURNS

I did not say this meat was tough. I just said I didn't see the horse that usually stands outside.

W. C. FIELDS

A rule of thumb in the matter of medical advice is to take everything any doctor says with a grain of aspirin.

GOODMAN ACE

For that tired, run-down feeling, try jaywalking.

My son has taken up meditation—at least it's better than sitting around doing nothing.

Memory is a marvelous thing—it enables you to remember a mistake each time you repeat it.

MAX KAUFFMANN

Man, an ingenious assembly of portable plumbing.

CHRISTOPHER MORLEY.

A good storyteller is a person who has a good memory and hopes other people haven't.

On one issue at least, men and women agree: They both distrust women.

H. L. MENCKEN

Any man who can't stand his wife lecturing to him
might find it a little easier to take sitting down.

IRVIN S. COBB

All a man has to do to become a millionaire in America is
invent a low-calorie diet that tastes good to eat.

Miami Beach is where neon goes to die.

LENNY BRUCE

A perfect example of minority rule is a pretty girl
surrounded by men.

A miser is a guy who lives within his income.
He's also called a magician.

ALLISTON (ONTARIO) HERALD

In order to profit from your mistakes, you
have to get out and make some.

LEROY B. HOUGHTON

The man who boasts he never made a mistake is
often married to a woman who did.

Money may not buy friends, but it certainly gives you
a better class of enemies.

If you have money, you are wise and good-looking and
can sing well, too.

Two can live as cheaply as one—and today they have to.

The movie was so bad, people were standing in line
to get out.

Everybody is a potential murderer. I've never killed anyone,
but I frequently get satisfaction reading the obituary notices.

CLARENCE DARROW

If there is a wrong way to do something, then
someone will do it.

EDWARD A. MURPHY

Sometimes the difference between a good speaker and
a poor speaker is a nice nap.

Neckties strangle clear thinking.

LIN YUTANG

Most of us are pretty good at postponing our
nervous breakdowns till we can afford them.

New York is like granola: Take away the fruits and nuts, and
all you have are the flakes.

I read the newspaper avidly.
It is my one form of continuous fiction.

ANEURIN BEVAN

So I became a newspaperman. I hated to do it but
I couldn't find honest employment.

MARK TWAIN

He had been kicked in the head by a mule when young and
believed everything he read in the Sunday papers.

GEORGE ADE

Don't get annoyed if your neighbor plays his hi-fi at
two o'clock in the morning.
Call him at four, and tell him how much you enjoyed it.

Old people shouldn't eat health foods.
They need all the preservatives they can get.

ROBERT ORBEN

There is no opinion so absurd that some philosopher
will not express it.

CICERO

You never know how absurd your own opinion is until you
hear somebody else quoting it.

An optimist is a man who will wink at a pretty girl and
think that his wife won't see him.

An optimist is a man who hurries because he thinks
his date is waiting for him.

Have a place for everything and keep the thing somewhere
else; this is not advice, it is merely custom.

MARK TWAIN

At six I was left an orphan. What on earth is a six-year-old
supposed to do with an orphan?

Do not do unto others as you would have them do unto you—
their tastes might not be the same.

GEORGE BERNARD SHAW

Now, owls are not really wise—they only look that way.
The owl is a sort of college professor.

ELBERT HUBBARD

People are like plants—some go to seed with age, and
others to pot.

When we have a pet peeve, it's remarkable how
often we pet it.

Prosperity can be a curse—especially if your neighbors have it.

The average Ph.D. thesis is nothing but the transference of
bones from one graveyard to another.

J. FRANK DOBIE

If you steal from one author it's plagiarism; if you steal from
many, it's research.

WILSON MIZNER

Adam was the only man who, when he said a good thing,
knew that nobody had said it before him.

MARK TWAIN

Hardly any woman reaches the age of thirty without
having been asked to marry at least twice—once
by her father, once by her mother.

A psychiatrist is a fellow who asks you a lot of expensive
questions your wife asks you for nothing.

JOEY ADAMS

I do not have a psychiatrist, and I do not want one, for
the simple reason that if he listened to me long enough, he
might become disturbed.

JAMES THURBER

A neurotic is a man who builds a castle in the air.
A psychotic is the man who lives in it.
And a psychiatrist is the man who collects the rent.

LORD WEBB JOHNSON

You go to a psychiatrist when you're slightly cracked and keep going until you're completely broke.

Mad money is the fee charged by a psychiatrist.

Roses are red, violets are blue; I'm schizophrenic, and so am I.

FRANK CROW

Neurotic means he is not as sensible as I am, and psychotic means that he is even worse than my brother-in-law.

KARL MENNINGER

Claustrophobia? It's a dreadful fear of Santa Claus.

VINNIE BARBARINO

You're never alone with schizophrenia.

A psychotic thinks that 2 + 2 = 5.
A neurotic *knows* that 2 + 2 = 4—he just can't stand it.

The trouble with the rat race is that
even if you win, you're still a rat.

LILY TOMLIN

It's a recession when your neighbor loses his job; it's a depression when you lose yours.

HARRY S. TRUMAN

A recession is a period during which you discover how much money you were wasting on nonessentials.

Chinese food: You do not sew with a fork, and
I see no reason why you should eat
with knitting needles.

MISS PIGGY

Retirement means twice as much husband on
half as much money.

A chrysanthemum by any other name would be easier to spell.

WILLIAM J. JOHNSTON

You are not permitted to kill a woman
who has injured you, but nothing forbids you to reflect that
she is growing older every minute. You are avenged
1,440 times a day.

AMBROSE BIERCE

The greatest luxury of riches is that they enable you to escape
so much good advice.

SIR ARTHUR HELPS

What's worse than an octopus with tennis elbow?
A centipede with athlete's foot.

Rowe's Rule: The odds are five to six that the light at the end
of the tunnel is the headlight of an oncoming train.

PAUL DICKSON

In the first place God made idiots. This was for practice.
Then He made school boards.

MARK TWAIN

When science finishes getting man up to the moon, maybe
it can have another try at getting pigeons
down from public buildings.

CHANGING TIMES

I do most of my work sitting down; that's where I shine.

ROBERT BENCHLEY

About the only way anybody can be shocked today is
by being hit by a bolt of lightning.

Many people buy on time, but only a few pay that way.

The fact that silence is golden may explain why
there is so little of it.

I can't sing. As a singist I am not a success.
I am saddest when I sing. So are those who hear me.
They are sadder even than I am.

CHARLES FARRAR BROWNE

Most people spend their lives going to bed when
they're not sleepy and getting up when they are!

CINDY ADAMS

I will grant, here, that I have stopped smoking now and then,
for a few months at a time, but it was not on principle, it was
only to show off; it was to pulverize those critics who said I
was a slave to my habits and couldn't break my bonds.

MARK TWAIN

To cease smoking is the easiest thing I ever did; I
ought to know because I've done it a thousand times.

MARK TWAIN

As ye smoke, so shall ye reek.

Laugh, and the world laughs with you; snore, and
you sleep alone.

MRS. PATRICK CAMPBELL

The good Samaritan for sociologists: A man was attacked and left
bleeding in a ditch. Two sociologists passed by, and one said to
the other, "We must find the man who did this—he needs help."

No sound is more pleasing to the human ear than the sound of
someone admitting that you're right.

I like the way you always manage to state the obvious with a
sense of real discovery.

GORE VIDAL

If I ever needed a brain transplant, I'd choose a sportswriter
because I'd want a brain that had never been used.

NORM VAN BROCKLIN

There are only two occasions when Americans respect privacy,
especially in presidents. Those are prayer and fishing.
So that some have taken to fishing.

HERBERT HOOVER

As a nation we are dedicated to keeping physically fit—and
parking as close to the stadium as possible.

BILL VAUGHAN

He was good-natured, obliging, and immensely ignorant and
was endowed with a stupidity which by the least little stretch
would go around the globe four times and tie.

MARK TWAIN

There's no secret about success. Did you ever know a
successful man that didn't tell you all about it?

KIN HUBBARD

If at first you don't succeed, you may be at
your level of incompetence already.

LAURENCE J. PETER

Success: the one unpardonable sin against one's fellows.

AMBROSE BIERCE

When someone says they have endured untold suffering,
you're about to hear it.

I feel like such a failure.
I've been shopping for over twenty years, and
I still have nothing to wear.

Tact is the ability to wish your relatives goodbye and convince
them that you're not happy to see them go.

The trouble with take-home pay today is that it turns out to
be just about enough to get you there.

I figured why Uncle Sam wears such a tall hat.
It comes in handy when he passes it around.

SOUPY SALES

With the state the world is in, any government could raise
unlimited revenue simply by taxing sins.

Whoever said you can't take it with you must have been an
Internal Revenue agent.

The three R's of the I. R. S.:
This is ours, that is ours, everything is ours.

Save your pennies; the dollars go to the I. R. S.

You have reached the _____ family. What you hear is the
barking of our killer Doberman pinscher, Wolf.
Please leave a message after the tone.

Television—a medium. So called because it is neither rare nor
well done.

ERNIE KOVACS

Television has done much for psychiatry by spreading information about it, as well as contributing to the need for it.

ALFRED HITCHCOCK

Don't worry about avoiding temptation—as you grow older, it starts avoiding you.
I didn't like the play, but then I saw it under adverse conditions: The curtain was up.

GROUCHO MARX

The only reason some people get lost in thought is because it's unfamiliar territory.

PAUL FIX

I am no athlete, but at one sport I used to be an expert. It was a dangerous game called "jumping to conclusions."

EDDIE CANTOR

When a man sits with a pretty girl for an hour, it seems like a minute. But let him sit on a hot stove for a minute—and it's longer than any hour. That's relativity.

ALBERT EINSTEIN

Some of the laziest people I know are the world's best clock watchers.

Tolerance is the ability to listen to another person tell you one of your best jokes.

Tolerance is the ability to listen to a person describe the same ailment you have.

Tourists are alike: They all want to go places where there are no tourists.

When most people put in their two cents' worth, they
aren't overcharging.

It was prettily devised of Aesop: The fly sat upon the axle-tree
of the chariot wheel and said, "What a dust I do raise!"

FRANCIS BACON

I'd complain about the service if I could find
a waiter to complain to.

MEL CALMAN

I love to go to Washington—if only to be near my money.

BOB HOPE

If I wanted to go crazy, I would do it in Washington
because it would not be noticed.

IRWIN S. COBB

The music at a wedding procession always reminds me of the
music of soldiers going into battle.

HEINRICH HEINE

We're having a little disagreement. What I want is a
big church wedding with bridesmaids and flowers and
a no-expense-spared reception, and what he wants is
to break off our engagement.

SALLY POPLIN

Wit makes its own welcome and levels all distinctions.
No dignity, no learning, no force of character can make
any stand against good wit.

RALPH WALDO EMERSON

Wit is the salt of conversation, not the food.

WILLIAM HAZLITT

Impropriety is the soul of wit.

W. SOMERSET MAUGHAM

Wit has truth in it; wisecracking is simply
calisthenics with words.

DOROTHY PARKER

In America the young are always ready to give to those
who are older than themselves the full benefits of
their inexperience.

OSCAR WILDE

A youthful figure is what you get when you ask
a women her age.

An abnormal person is anyone who behaves
differently from you.

You can pick out the actors by the glazed look that
comes into their eyes when the conversation wanders
away from themselves.

MICHAEL WILDING

The most important thing in acting is honesty.
If you can fake that, you've got it made.

GEORGE BURNS

"Frank and explicit"—that is the right line to take when
you wish to conceal your own mind and to confuse
the minds of others.

BENJAMIN DISRAELI

Do you know the difference between a beautiful woman and
a charming one? A beauty is a woman you notice; a
charmer is one who notices you.

ADLAI STEVENSON

A conference is a gathering of important people who
singly can do nothing, but together can decide
that nothing can be done.

FRED ALLEN

Cricket is a game which the British, not being
a spiritual people, had to invent in order to have
some concept of eternity.

LORD MANCROFT

The motivation that makes some women keep in
shipshape is other women who are seeworthy.

The difference between genius and stupidity is
that genius has its limits.

A gentleman is one who never hurts
anyone's feelings unintentionally.

OLIVER HERFORD

A gentleman is a man who has trained himself to yawn in
such a way that you think he is smiling at you.

The one human characteristic that can make a person
stand out above all other in a group is a mannerism
of complete gentleness.

If you can keep your head when all about you are losing theirs,
perhaps you have misunderstood the situation.

GRAFFITO

Try praising your wife even if it does frighten her at first.

BILLY SUNDAY

Some people pay a compliment as if they expected a receipt.

KIN HUBBARD

Dear Sir,
　　Your profession has, as usual, destroyed your brain.

GEORGE BERNARD SHAW

A woman shopping in a department store noticed that the clerk behind the complaint desk smiled at everyone who talked to her and kept her voice low and pleasant, even when irate customers spoke rudely to her. The shopper was amazed at the way the woman kept her cool. Then she noticed the clerk's dark earrings. On one, in white lettering, was inscribed, "In" and on the other, "Out."

Better a witty fool than a foolish wit.

WILLIAM SHAKESPEARE

LEADERSHIP

The supreme quality for leadership
is unquestionably integrity. Without it,
no real success is possible, no matter
whether it is on a section gang, a
football field, in an army,
or in an office.

DWIGHT D. EISENHOWER

If anything goes bad, I did it.
If anything goes semi-good, then we did it.
If anything goes real good, then you did it.
That's all it takes to get people to win football games for you.

BEAR BRYANT

Rarely is a fight continued when the chief has fallen.

Get into the habit of asking yourself if what you're doing can
be handled by someone else.

Fail to honor people, they fail to honor you.
But of a good leader, who talks little, when his work is done,
his aim fulfilled, they will all say, "We did this ourselves."

LAO-TSE

As a manager you're paid to be uncomfortable. If you're
comfortable, it's a sure sign you're doing things wrong.

PETER DRUCKER

The very essence of all power to influence lies in
getting the other person to participate.

HARRY A. OVERSTREET

A great leader never sets himself above his followers
except in carrying responsibilities.

JULES ORMONT

It is the capacity to develop and improve their skills
that distinguishes leaders from their followers.

WARREN BENNIS AND BERT NANUS

The best leader is the one who has the sense to
surround himself with outstanding people and the
self-restraint not to meddle with how they do their jobs.

A good leader inspires other men with confidence in him; a
great leader inspires them with confidence in themselves.

When a leader makes a mistake, all the people suffer.

There are two kinds of leaders in the world—some are
interested in the fleece, others in the flock.

The question "Who ought to be boss?" is like asking
"Who ought to be the tenor in the quartet?"
Obviously, the man who can sing tenor.

HENRY FORD

Divorced from ethics, leadership is reduced to management
and politics to mere technique.

JAMES MACGREGOR BURNS

There are no office hours for leaders.

CARDINAL GIBBONS

Trust is the emotional glue that binds followers
and leaders together.

WARREN BENNIS AND BERT NANUS

Nearly all men can stand adversity, but if you want to
test a man's character, give him power.

ABRAHAM LINCOLN

Power may justly be compared to a great river; while
kept within its bounds it is both beautiful and useful, but
when it overflows its banks, it brings destruction and
desolation to all in its way.

ANDREW HAMILTON

Power for good flows through you from God.
It does not originate with you.

W. F. SMITH

Communicate downward to subordinates with
at least the same care and attention as you communicate
upward to superiors.

L. B. BELKER

To get people to follow the straight and narrow path, stop
giving them advice and start leading the way.

The higher the ape climbs the more he shows his rump.

An army of a thousand is easy to find, but, ah, how
difficult to find a general.

Where the chief walks, there questions are decided.

Give your decisions, never your reasons; your decisions
may be right, but your reasons are sure to wrong.

WILLIAM MURRAY

A decision is what a man makes when he can't get
anyone to serve on a committee.

FLETCHER KNEBEL

My rule, in which I have always found satisfaction, is, never turn aside in public affairs through views of private interest; but to go straight forward in doing what appears to me right at the time, leaving the consequences with Providence.

BENJAMIN FRANKLIN

Your decisions will always be better if you do what is right for the organization rather than what is right for yourself.

It is the practice of the multitude to bark at eminent men, as little dogs do at strangers.

SENECA

One of the first things that every top executive learns is that a very high percentage of his salary goes just to pay him to listen.

Don't fight the problem; decide it.

GENERAL GEORGE C. MARSHALL

I cannot give you the formula for success, but I can give you the formula for failure, which is: Try to please everybody.

HERBERT BAYARD SWOPE

When a subordinate is not performing adequately, rather than firing the person outright, some responsibility and authority are removed in the hope that the individual will be able to perform better with fewer responsibilities. Fairness and human dignity are preserved when this first step is employed; it gives the unsatisfactory performer a chance to "turn it around." If behavior and performance are not reversed, the next step is to get the individual out of the decision-making process as much as possible. Having the person report to another superior is a good way to do it.

DONALD T. PHILLIPS

Men make history and not the other way round. In periods where there is no leadership, society stands still. Progress occurs when courageous, skillful leaders seize the opportunity to change things for the better.

HARRY S. TRUMAN

I am compelled to take a more impartial and unprejudiced view of things. Without claiming to be your superior, which I do not, my position enables me to understand my duty in all these matters better than you possibly can, and I hope you do not yet doubt my integrity.

ABRAHAM LINCOLN

When the conduct of men is designed to be influenced, persuasion—kind, unassuming persuasion—should ever be adopted. It is an old and a true maxim, that a "drop of honey catches more flies than a gallon of gall." So with men. If you would win a man to your cause, first convince him that you are his sincere friend. Therein is a drop of honey that catches his heart, which, say what he will, is the great high road to his reason, and which, when once gained, you will find but little trouble in convincing his judgment of the justice of your cause, if indeed that cause really be a just one. On the contrary, assume to dictate to his judgment or to command his action or to mark him as one to be shunned and despised, and he will retreat within himself, close all the avenues to his head and his heart; and, though your cause be naked truth itself, . . . you shall no more be able to [reach] him, than to penetrate the hard shell of a tortoise with a rye straw.

Such is man, and so must he be understood by those who would lead him, even to his own best interest.

ABRAHAM LINCOLN

It takes a great man to make a good listener.

SIR ARTHUR HELPS

The pioneers in any movement are not generally the best people to carry that movement to a successful issue. They often have to meet such hard opposition, and get so battered and bespattered, that afterward, when people find they have to accept reform, they will accept it more easily from others.

ABRAHAM LINCOLN

An institution is the lengthened shadow of one man . . . and all history resolves itself very easily into the biography of a few stout and earnest persons.

RALPH WALDO EMERSON

He that has not served knows not how to command.

Our chief want in life is somebody who shall
make us do what we can.

In this world a man must either be anvil or hammer.

HENRY W. LONGFELLOW

LOVE

Love is not blind—it sees more,
not less. But because it sees more,
it is willing to see less.

JULIUS GORDON

Absence is to love what wind is to fire; it puts out
the little, it kindles the great.

ROGER DE BUSSY-RABUTIN

You've got to love what's lovable and hate what's hateable.
It takes brains to see the difference.

ROBERT FROST

Love's best habit is a soothing tongue.

WILLIAM SHAKESPEARE

Nothing spoils the taste of peanut butter like unrequited love.

CHARLIE BROWN

Love does not dominate; it cultivates.

GOETHE

There is no greater invitation to love than loving first.

SAINT AUGUSTINE

The last time I saw Fay he was walking down Lovers' Lane,
holding his own hand.

FRED ALLEN

'Tis impossible to love and be wise.

FRANCIS BACON

Faults are thick where love is thin.

Love is like the measles; we can have it but once, and the later in life we have it, the tougher it goes with us.

JOSH BILLINGS

Love's a malady without a cure.

JOHN DRYDEN

Love often makes a fool of the cleverest men, and as often gives cleverness to the most foolish.

Love is like the measles; we all have to go through it.

JEROME K. JEROME

He gave her a look you could have poured on a waffle.

RING LARDNER

Love is the delusion that one woman differs from another.

H. L. MENCKEN

Woman begins by resisting a man's advances and ends by blocking his retreat.

OSCAR WILDE

Love is like the five loaves and fishes.
It doesn't start to multiply until you give it away.

INSPIRATIONAL THOUGHTS

Love does not die easily. It is a living thing.
It thrives in the face of all life's hazards, save one—neglect.

JAMES D. BRYDEN

Love at first sight is possible, but it always pays
to take a second look.

The love that passeth all understanding is on television.

The arithmetic of love is unique: Two halves do not make
a whole; only two wholes make a whole.

JO COUDERT

You might as well withdraw love as threaten to withdraw it; to
one who loves you, these are equal catastrophes.

If Jack's in love, he's no judge of Jill's beauty.

BENJAMIN FRANKLIN

Love is the free exercise of choice. Two people love each other
only when they are quite capable of living without each other
but choose to live with each other.

M. SCOTT PECK

You can always try to teach people to love you in your style, but
never expect anyone, no matter how close, to read your mind
and heart. Tell them what you want. The investment you make
in surprise is often a hidden expectation that brings disappoint-
ment. Better yet, buy yourself your heart's desire. Don't turn
special days into tests of love. Take care of yourself in the style
you prefer—yours. Then, anything else you receive on that day
will seem like extra love that you can enjoy without hurtful
expectations.

JENNIFER JAMES

He who covers over an offense promotes love, but
whoever repeats the matter separates close friends.

PROVERBS 17:9

Men are taught that women respect them for their strength
and that may well be true, but they love them for
their vulnerability.

MERLE SHAIN

He prayeth best who loveth best.

SAMUEL TAYLOR COLERIDGE

MATURITY

The following qualities are criteria
of emotional maturity: the ability
to deal constructively with reality,
the capacity to adapt to change,
relative freedom from symptoms
produced by tensions and anxieties,
the capacity to find more satisfaction
in giving than receiving, the capacity
to relate to others in a consistent
manner with mutual satisfaction
and helpfulness, the capacity to
sublimate, the capacity to love.

WILLIAM C. MENNIGER

Age is like love; it cannot be hid.

THOMAS DEKKER

The older I grow, the more I distrust the familiar
doctrine that age brings wisdom.

H. L. MENCKEN

The years that a woman subtracts from her age are not lost.
They are added to the ages of other women.

DIANE DE POITIERS

I'll tell ya how to stay young: Hang around with older people.

BOB HOPE

You know you're getting older when the happy hour is a nap.

I am long on ideas, but short on time.

I expect to live to be only about a hundred.

THOMAS EDISON

Of all the faculties of the human mind, that of memory
is the first which suffers from age.

THOMAS JEFFERSON

When a man is young, he is so wild he is insufferable.
When he is old, he plays the saint and
becomes insufferable again.

NIKOLAI GOGOL

The secret of staying young is to live honestly,
eat slowly, and
lie about your age.

LUCILLE BALL

The only good thing about it [aging] is you're not dead.

LILLIAN HELLMAN

Age is so deceiving. It is amazing how much faster
sixty comes after fifty compared to fifty after forty!

To be seventy years young is sometimes far more cheerful and
hopeful than to be forty years old.

Age does not give sense, it only makes one go slowly.

When you're over the hill, you pick up speed.

Age is a question of mind over matter.
If you don't mind, it doesn't matter.

SATCHEL PAIGE

PERSEVERANCE

Never give in, never give in, never,
never, never, never—in nothing, great
or small, large or petty—never give
in except to convictions of honor
and good sense.

WINSTON CHURCHILL

Even the woodpecker owes his success to the fact
that he uses his head and keeps pecking away
until he finishes the job he starts.

COLEMAN COX

Most people give up just when they're about to
achieve success. They quit on the one-yard line.
They give up at the last minute of the game one foot from a
winning touchdown.

H. ROSS PEROT

The will to persevere is often the difference between
failure and success.

DAVID SARNOFF

Nothing in the world can take the place of persistence. Talent
will not; nothing is more common than unsuccessful men with
talent. Genius will not; unrewarded genius is almost a proverb.
Education will not; the world is full of educated derelicts. Persistence and determination are omnipotent. The slogan "press
on" has solved and always will solve the problems of the human
race.

CALVIN COOLIDGE

Perseverance is not a long race; it is many short races
one after another.

WALTER ELLIOTT

When things go wrong, as they sometimes will,
When the road you're trudging seems all uphill,
When care is pressing you down a bit,
Rest, if you must—but don't you quit.
Often the goal is nearer than it seems to a faint and faltering
    man;
Often the struggler has given up
When he might have captured the victor's cup.
Press on.

PRACTICAL THOUGHTS

There is nothing in the world more
powerful than an idea. No weapon can
destroy it; no power can conquer it
except the power of another idea.

JAMES ROY SMITH

Abstract art? A product of the untalented, sold by
the unprincipled to the utterly bewildered.

AL CAPP

Some of the greatest love affairs I've ever known
involved one actor, unassisted.

I deny I ever said that actors are cattle. What I said was,
"Actors should be treated like cattle."

ALFRED HITCHCOCK

Ignorance is the mother of admiration.

GEORGE CHAPMAN

Advertising is a racket . . . its constructive contribution to
humanity is exactly minus zero.

F. SCOTT FITZGERALD

Admiration: our polite recognition of another's
resemblance to ourselves.

Alimony: bounty after the mutiny.

MAX KAUFFMANN

He is a sheep in sheep's clothing.

WINSTON CHURCHILL

He bears an unmistakable resemblance to a cornered rat.

NORMAN MAILER

Ah, don't say that you agree with me. When people agree
with me, I always feel that I must be wrong.

OSCAR WILDE

Always make the audience suffer as much as possible.

ALFRED HITCHCOCK

The trouble with being bald is not so much in combing
your hair as in knowing where to draw the line
when you wash your face.

Billy the Kid: a nondescript, adenoidal, weasel-eyed,
narrow-chested, stoop-shouldered, repulsive-looking creature
with all the outward appearance of a cretin.

BURTON RASCOE

A bore is a fellow who opens his mouth and puts his feats in it.

HENRY FORD

Broadly speaking, human beings may be divided into three
classes: those who are billed to death, those who are worried to
death, and those who are bored to death.

WINSTON CHURCHILL

Boston is a moral and intellectual nursery, always busy
applying first principles to trifles.

GEORGE SANTAYANA

A boy is an appetite with a skin pulled over it.

Assassination is the extreme form of censorship.

GEORGE BERNARD SHAW

He has all the characteristics of a dog—except loyalty.

SAM HOUSTON (SPEAKING ABOUT THOMAS JEFFERSON GREEN)

We failed, but in the good providence of God, apparent failure often proves a blessing.

ROBERT E. LEE

What is a committee? A group of the unwilling, picked from the unfit, to do the unnecessary.

RICHARD HARKNESS

The difference between news and gossip lies in whether you raise your voice or lower it.

FRANKLIN P. JONES

A quarrelsome wife is like a constant dripping on a rainy day; restraining her is like restraining the wind or grasping oil with the hand.

PROVERBS 27:15-16

Today a murderer is assumed innocent until proven insane.

Critics are like pigs at the pastry cart.

JOHN UPDIKE

A critic is someone who never actually goes to the battle yet who afterwards comes out shooting the wounded.

TYNE DALY

Critics are a dissembling, dishonest, contemptible race of men. Asking a working writer what he thinks about critics is like asking a lamppost what it feels about dogs.

JOHN OSBORNE

I have just read your lousy review. You sound like a frustrated old man who never made a success, an eight-ulcer man on a four-ulcer job . . . I have never met you, but if I do, you'll need a new nose, a lot of beefsteak for black eyes, and a supporter below.

HARRY S. TRUMAN

The cynic is one who never sees a good quality in a man, and never fails to see a bad one. He is the human owl, vigilant in darkness, and blind to light, mousing for vermin, and never see-ing noble game.

HENRY WARD BEECHER

There's a little country in all of us, a little frontier.

LOUIS L'AMOUR

A cynic is a man who, when he smells flowers, looks
around for a coffin.

H. L. MENCKEN

He is useless on top of the ground; he ought to be under it,
inspiring the cabbages.

MARK TWAIN

The devil is an optimist if he thinks he can
make people meaner.

KARL KRAUS

We are so fond of each other because our ailments
are the same.

JONATHAN SWIFT

One of the greatest pieces of charlatanic, and satanic,
nonsense imposed on a gullible public is the
Freudian interpretation of dreams.

VLADIMIR NABOKOV

He who has the reputation of rising early may sleep till noon.
FRENCH PROVERB

He is a self-made man, and worships his creator.
JOHN BRIGHT

Arrogant, pompous, obnoxious, vain, cruel, persecuting,
distasteful, verbose, a show-off.
I have been called all of these. Of course, I am.
HOWARD COSELL

Talk to a man about himself and he will listen for hours.
BENJAMIN DISRAELI

Edith was a little country bounded on the north,
south, east, and west by Edith.
MARTHA OSTENSO

When a man is wrapped up in himself, he makes
a pretty small package.
JOHN RUSKIN

Egotist, n. A person more interested in himself than in me.
AMBROSE BIERCE

Many problems in business are caused by
the ego interfering with judgment.

I do desire we may be better strangers.
WILLIAM SHAKESPEARE

I'm lonesome. They are all dying.
I have hardly a warm personal enemy left.
J. A. MCNEILL WHISTLER

He who is feared by many, fears many.

Taking to pieces is the trade of those who cannot construct.

RALPH WALDO EMERSON

A cynic is a man who knows the price of everything, and
the value of nothing.

OSCAR WILDE

I don't have a warm personal enemy left. They've all died off.
I miss them terribly because they helped define me.

CLARE BOOTHE LUCE

In order to appreciate England one has to have
a certain contempt for logic.

LIN YUTANG

It is a wise man who said that there is no greater inequality
than the equal treatment of unequals.

FELIX FRANKFURTER

There is no more reason to believe that man descended from
some inferior animal than there is to believe that a stately
mansion has descended from a small cottage.

WILLIAM JENNINGS BRYAN

Any excuse will serve a tyrant.

AESOP

He reminds me of the man who murdered both his parents,
and then, when sentence was about to be pronounced, pleaded
for mercy on the grounds that he was an orphan.

ABRAHAM LINCOLN

You have such a February face,
So full of frost, of storm, and cloudiness.

WILLIAM SHAKESPEARE

He had the sort of face that, once seen, is never remembered.

OSCAR WILDE

One of the quickest ways to feel tired is
to suppress your feelings.

SUE PATTON THOEK

Never argue with a fool—people might not know
the difference.

FIRST LAW OF DEBATE

I know of no way of judging the future but by the past.

PATRICK HENRY

Like a lame man's legs that hang limp is a proverb in the
mouth of a fool.

PROVERBS 26:7

If a wise man goes to court with a fool, the fool rages and
scoffs, and there is no peace.

PROVERBS 29:9

Young men think old men are fools, but old men
know young men are fools.

GEORGE CHAPMAN

I did not attend his funeral, but I wrote a nice letter
saying I approved of it.

MARK TWAIN

People who worry the most about the future are usually those
who are doing the least to prepare for it.

One thing I've discovered is that trees grow on money.

I never met a gardener who didn't know better
than other gardeners.

All generalizations are false, including this one.

Genius, in one respect, is like gold—numbers of persons are
constantly writing about both, who have neither.

C. C. COLTON

A brilliant man is one who is shrewd enough
to recognize you're a genius.

Like cold water to a weary soul is
good news from a distant land.

PROVERBS 25:25

Gossip is when you hear something you like
about someone you don't.

EARL WILSON

If you haven't got anything nice to say about anybody, come
sit next to me.

ALICE ROOSEVELT LONGWORTH

Without wood a fire goes out; without gossip a
quarrel dies down.

PROVERBS 26:20

A gossip betrays a confidence; so avoid a man
who talks too much.

PROVERBS 20:19

Gossip is like coal: If it does not char, at least it will blacken.

Gossip is a form of malicious talk indulged in by other people.

Gossip is what you hear; news is what you tell.

No matter how outstanding teamwork may be in accomplishing something great, history will identify it with a single name years or centuries later.

Gumperson's Law: The probability of anything happening is in inverse ratio to its desirability.

JOHN W. HAZARD

Not ten yoke of oxen
Have the power to draw us
Like a woman's hair!

HENRY W. LONGFELLOW

A hypochondriac is one who has a pill for everything except what ails him.

They call him "Jigsaw" because every time he's faced with a problem, he goes to pieces.

India is no more a political personality than Europe.
India is a geographical term.
It is no more a united nation than the equator.

WINSTON CHURCHILL

Journalism largely consists in saying, "Lord Jones Dead" to people who never knew Lord Jones was alive.

G. K. CHESTERTON

The only qualities for real success in journalism are ratlike cunning, a plausible manner, and a little literary ability.
The capacity to steal other people's ideas and phrases . . .
is also invaluable.

NICHOLAS TOMALIN

King Heroin is my shepherd; I shall always want. He maketh me to lie down in the gutters. He leadeth me beside the troubled waters. He destroyeth my soul. He leadeth me in the paths of wickedness for the effort's sake. Yea, I shall walk through the valley of poverty and will fear all evil, for thou, Heroin, art with me. Thy needle and capsule try to comfort me. Thou strippest the table of groceries in the presence of my family. Thou robbest my head of reason. My cup of sorrow runneth over. Surely heroin addiction shall stalk me all the days of my life and I will dwell in the house of the damned forever.

The Peter Principle: In a hierarchy every employee tends to rise to his level of incompetence.

LAWRENCE J. PETER

Win your lawsuit, and lose your money.

Libraries are the marketplaces of human thought.

TREVOR FAWCETT

Life is a foreign language; all men mispronounce it.

CHRISTOPHER MORLEY

Tact is the ability to make a person see the lightning without letting him feel the bolt.

Lincoln is one of those peculiar men who perform with admirable skill everything which they undertake.

STEPHEN A. DOUGLAS

Not often in the story of mankind does a man arrive on earth who is both steel and velvet, who is as hard as rock and soft as drifting fog, who holds in his heart and mind the paradox of terrible storm and peace unspeakable and perfect.

CARL SANDBURG

Literature is a very bad crutch but a very good walking stick.

CHARLES LAMB

Man is stumbling blindly through a spiritual darkness while toying with the precarious secrets of life and death. The world has achieved brilliance without wisdom, power without conscience. We know more about war than we know about peace, more about killing than we know about living.

GENERAL OMAR BRADLEY

Men who can speak a number of different tongues are notorious for having little to say in any of them.

H. R. HUSE

Some people look for faults as if they were buried treasure.

The beauty of memory is that it still sees beauty
when beauty has faded.

PAUL BOESE

There is nothing like an odor to stir memories.

WILLIAM MCFEE

Man is the only animal that can remain on friendly terms with the victims he intends to eat until he eats them.

SAMUEL BUTLER

In youth, everything seems possible, but we reach a point in the middle years when we realize that we are never going to reach all the shining goals we had set for ourselves. And in the end, most of us reconcile ourselves, with what grace we can, to living with our ulcers and arthritis, our sense of partial failure, our less-than-ideal families—and even our politicians!

ADLAI STEVENSON

The worst thing about middle age is that you outgrow it.

One of the chief pleasures of middle age is looking back at the people you didn't marry.

Middle age is when a man figures he has enough financial security to wear the flashy sports coats he didn't have the courage to wear when he was young.

BILL VAUGHAN

Middle age is when your age starts to show around your middle.

BOB HOPE

Middle age is when you are impressed not with the fact that the grass is greener on the other side of the fence but rather how difficult the fence looks to get over.

NORTH VERNON SUN

Middle age is the time of life when the fellow who always acted like a human dynamo starts showing signs of ignition trouble.

Middle age is when you hope nobody will invite you out next Saturday night.

Middle age is when you burn the midnight oil around 9 p.m.

Middle age is when your narrow waist and broad mind begin to change places.

It's called "middle age" because that's where it shows.

Middle age has arrived when a man's idea of get-up-and-go is to go to bed.

Middle age is the time of life when a man starts blaming the cleaners because his suits are shrinking.

A liberal mind is a mind that is able to imagine itself believing anything.

MAX EASTMAN

A miserable person is one who insists on sharing his misery with you.

The love of money is a root of all kinds of evil.

I TIMOTHY 6:10

The man who makes no mistakes does not usually make anything.

WILLIAM CONNOR MAGEE

All assemblages of men are different from the men themselves. Neither intelligence nor culture can prevent a man from acting as a mob. The wise man and the knave lose their identity and merge themselves into a new being.

THOMAS BRACKETT REED

Money lays waste cities; it sets men to roaming from home; it seduces and corrupts honest men and turns virtue to baseness; it teaches villainy and impiety.

SOPHOCLES

Here's to our town—a place where people spend money they haven't earned to buy things they don't need to impress people they don't like.

LEWIS C. HENRY

A fool may make money, but it needs a wise man to spent it.

CHARLES H. SPURGEON

It takes lots of money to make ends meet nowadays—as a matter of fact, it takes twice as much.

Chains of gold are stronger than chains of iron.

He that does lend does lose his money and friend.

Money is a good servant but a bad master.

Money can't buy happiness—but then, happiness
can't buy groceries.

Money can talk, but it doesn't hear very well when you call it.

Soon gotten, soon spent.

If the man and woman walk away together at the end of the
picture, it adds $10 million to the box office.

GEORGE LUCAS

You make as good music as a wheelbarrow.

THOMAS FULLER

The men that women marry, and why they marry them, will
always be a marvel and a mystery to the world.

HENRY W. LONGFELLOW

A narcissist is someone better looking than you are.

GORE VIDAL

He fell in love with himself at first sight, and it is a
passion to which he has always remained faithful.

ANTHONY POWELL

New Yorkers now see only what they want to see.
The bodies don't bother them; they step around them.

NICOLE LAURIER

Must is a king's word.

The man who never looks into a newspaper is better informed than he who reads them; inasmuch as he who knows nothing is nearer to truth than he whose mind is filled with falsehoods and errors. He who reads nothing will still learn the great facts, and the details are all false.

THOMAS JEFFERSON

Advertisements contain the only truths to be relied on in a newspaper.

THOMAS JEFFERSON

It is a melancholy truth, that a suppression of the press could not more completely deprive the nation of its benefits, than is done by its abandoned prostitution of falsehood. Nothing can now be believed which is seen in a newspaper.

THOMAS JEFFERSON

But let me beseech you, sir, not to let this letter get into a newspaper. Tranquillity, at my age, is the supreme good of life. I think it a duty, and it is my earnest wish, to take no further part in public affairs . . . The abuse of confidence by publishing my letters has cost me more than all other pains.

THOMAS JEFFERSON

All successful newspapers are ceaselessly querulous and bellicose. They never defend anyone or anything if they can help it; if the job is forced upon them, they tackle it by denouncing someone or something else.

H. L. MENCKEN

Journalists say a thing that they know isn't true, in the hope that if they keep on saying it long enough it will be true.

ARNOLD BENNETT

I do not take a single newspaper, nor read one a month, and I feel myself infinitely the happier for it.

THOMAS JEFFERSON

"The papers are not always reliable," Lincoln interjected, "that is to say, Mr. Welles, they lie and then they re-lie."

CARL SANDBURG

The mass media know their reports are worth nothing compared to the eye and voice of a serious writer. Like cowardly bulls, people in the mass media paw the ground when one comes near.

NORMAN MAILER

The art of newspaper paragraphing is to stroke a platitude until it purrs like an epigram.

DON MARQUIS

But implicit in the history of the First Amendment is the rejection of obscenity as utterly without redeeming social importance.

JUSTICE WILLIAM J. BRENNAN JR.

It's not miserable to be old; it's miserable not to be capable of living your age.

EUGENE P. BERTIN

Man fools himself. He prays for a long life, and he fears old age.

CHINESE PROVERB

Anyone can get old. All you have to do is live long enough.

GROUCHO MARX

Old age does not announce itself.

Now that I finally know my way around, I don't feel like going.

The way to live to be one hundred is to reach ninety-nine and then to live very carefully.

At sixty, you realize that grandfather wasn't so old when he died at eighty.

A man is never too old to learn, but he is sometimes too young.

One lesson we learn early—that in spite of seeming difference, men are all of one pattern. In fact, the only sin which we never forgive in each other is difference of opinion.

RALPH WALDO EMERSON

Fill your mouth with marbles, and make a speech.
Every day, reduce the number of marbles in your mouth, and make a speech. You will soon become an accredited public speaker—as soon as you have lost all your marbles.

BROOKS HAYS

There is no record in human history of a happy philosopher.

H. L. MENCKEN

Then he asked the question that you are all itching to ask me: "How can you tell good poetry from bad?" I answered, "How does one tell good fish from bad? Surely by the smell? Use your nose."

ROBERT GRAVES

Publishing a volume of verse is like dropping a rose petal down the Grand Canyon and waiting for the echo.

DON MARQUIS

Robert Creeley's poems have two main characteristics: (1) They are short; (2) they are not short enough.

JOHN SIMON

Peacock, look at your legs.

The man is either crazy or he is a poet.

HORACE

There is no such thing as a fixed policy because policy, like all organic entities, is always in the making.

LORD SALISBURY

The best way to help the poor is
not to become one of them.

LAING HANCOCK

The poor have more children, but the rich
have more relatives.

Pornography tells lies about women.
But pornography tells the truth about men.

JOHN STOLTENBERG

After being turned down by numerous publishers, he
decided to write for posterity.

GEORGE ADE

Poverty is no disgrace, but also no great honor.

Some people will say anything except their prayers.

HORACE WYNDHAM

Prejudice is never easy unless it can pass itself off for reason.

WILLIAM HAZLITT

A prejudiced person is one who doesn't believe
in the same things we do.

ART LINKLETTER

One may no more live in the world without
picking up the moral prejudices of the world than
one will be able to go to hell without perspiring.

H. L. MENCKEN

Racial prejudice is a pigment of the imagination.

GRAFFITO

An infallible method of conciliating a tiger is
to allow oneself to be devoured.

KONRAD ADENAUER

An appeaser is one who feeds a crocodile, hoping
it will eat him last.

WINSTON CHURCHILL

I'd like to buy him at my price and sell him at his.

It is easier to write ten volumes of philosophy than
to put one principle into practice.

LEO TOLSTOY

It is easier to fight for one's principles than
to live up to them.

ALFRED ADLER

It doesn't pay well to fight for what we believe in.

LILLIAN HELLMAN

The value of a principle is the number
of things it will explain.

RALPH WALDO EMERSON

Prison is a socialist's paradise, where equality prevails,
everything is supplied, and competition is eliminated.

ELBERT HUBBARD

If we work upon marble it will perish; if we work upon brass, time will efface it; if we rear temples, they will crumble into dust; but if we work upon immortal minds, if we imbue them with principles, with just the fear of God and love of our fellow men, we engrave on those tablets something which will brighten all eternity.

DANIEL WEBSTER

A prisoner of war is a man who tries to kill you and fails, and then asks you not to kill him.

WINSTON CHURCHILL

Is it progress if a cannibal uses knife and fork?

STANISLAW J. LEC

No man acquires property without acquiring with it a little arithmetic also.

RALPH WALDO EMERSON

He bade me have a care for the future, to make sure of the bear before I sell his skin.

The best way to get a puppy is to beg for a baby brother— they'll settle for a puppy every time.

WINSTON PENDELTON

Men are not flattered by being shown that there has been a difference of purpose between the Almighty and them.

ABRAHAM LINCOLN

He's been that way for years—a born questioner but he hates answers.

RING LARDNER

Men are not against you; they are merely for themselves.

GENE FOWLER

He has left off reading altogether, to the great
improvement of his originality.

CHARLES LAMB

Reality is when you find out that the boss did overhear
what you said about him.

Man does not live by words alone, despite the fact that sometimes he has to eat them.

ADLAI STEVENSON

I have always liked bird dogs better than kennel-fed dogs
myself—you know, one that will get out and hunt for food
rather than sit on his fanny and yell.

CHARLES E. WILSON

The most important sentence in any article is the first one. If it
doesn't induce the reader to proceed to the second sentence,
your article is dead. And if the second sentence doesn't induce
him to continue to the third sentence, it's equally dead. Of such
a progress of sentences, each tugging the reader forward until he
is safely hooked, a writer constructs that fateful unit: the "lead."

WILLIAM ZINSSER

No one knows better where the shoe pinches
than he who wears it.

Silence is the most perfect expression of scorn.

GEORGE BERNARD SHAW

An actor entering through the door, you've got nothing.
But if he enters through the window, you've got a situation.

BILLY WILDER

Whenever [I] hear anyone arguing for slavery, I feel a strong
impulse to see it tried on him personally.

ABRAHAM LINCOLN

There are three kinds of lies: lies, damned lies, and statistics.

MARK TWAIN

I am not going to be terrified by an excited populace, and hindered from speaking my honest sentiments upon this infernal subject of human slavery.

ABRAHAM LINCOLN

In this enlightened age, there are few, I believe, but what will acknowledge that slavery as an institution is a moral and political evil in any country.

ROBERT E. LEE

Although volume upon volume is written to prove slavery a very good thing, we never hear of the man who wishes to take the good of it by being a slave himself.

ABRAHAM LINCOLN

The ideal social state is not that in which each gets an equal amount of wealth, but in which each gets in proportion to his contribution to the general stock.

HENRY GEORGE

"Then you should say what you mean," the March Hare went on.

"I do," Alice hastily replied; "at least—at least I mean what I say—that's the same thing, you know."

"Not the same thing a bit!" said the Hatter. "Why, you might as well say 'I see what I eat' is the same thing as 'I eat what I see'!"

LEWIS CARROLL

In my present position, it is hardly proper for me to make speeches. Every word is so closely noted that it will not do to make trivial ones.

ABRAHAM LINCOLN

. . . the sort of play that gives failures a bad name.

WALTER KERR

I have never taken any exercise, except
for sleeping and resting, and I never intend to take any.
Exercise is loathsome.

MARK TWAIN

He uses statistics as a drunken man uses lampposts—for
support rather than for illumination.

ANDREW LANG

Tact is the ability to light a fire under a person
without having to apply a torch.

Tact is the ability not to describe others exactly as you see them.

Tactless people suffer from chronic indiscretion.

The power to tax is the power to destroy.

DANIEL WEBSTER

A teacher who is attempting to teach without inspiring the
pupil with a desire to learn is hammering on a cold iron.

HORACE MANN

A teacher affects eternity; he can never tell where
his influence stops.

HENRY ADAMS

He that hath a trade, hath an estate.

BENJAMIN FRANKLIN

He who has a trade may travel through the world.

With reasonable men, I will reason; with
humane men, I will plead; but
to tyrants I will give no quarter, nor
waste arguments where they will certainly be lost.

WILLIAM LLOYD GARRISON

We must all hang together, or assuredly we shall
all hang separately.

BENJAMIN FRANKLIN

University politics are vicious precisely because
the stakes are so small.

HENRY KISSINGER

Never underestimate a man who overestimates himself.

FRANKLIN D. ROOSEVELT

The more successful the villain, the
more successful the picture.

ALFRED HITCHCOCK

There is no longer any room for hope. If we wish to be free—if
we mean to preserve inviolate those inestimable privileges for
which we have been so long contending—if we mean not basely
to abandon the noble struggle in which we have been so long
engaged, and which we have pledged ourselves never to abandon, until the glorious object of our contest shall be
obtained—we must fight! I repeat it, sir, we must fight!! An
appeal to arms and to the God of Hosts, is all that is left us!

PATRICK HENRY

I must study politics and war that my sons may have
liberty to study mathematics and philosophy.

JOHN ADAMS

My first wish is to see this plague to mankind banished from off the earth, and the sons and daughters of this world employed in more pleasing and innocent amusements than in preparing implements and exercising them for the destruction of mankind.

GEORGE WASHINGTON

He who cannot stand the smell of gunpowder
should not engage in war.

There is many a boy here today who looks on war as all glory, but, boys, it is all hell. You can bear this warning voice to generations yet to come. I look upon war with horror.

WILLIAM T. SHERMAN

The four great motives which move men to social activity are hunger, love, vanity, and fear of superior powers. If we search out the causes which have moved men to war, we find them under each of these motives or interests.

WILLIAM GRAHAM SUMNER

[George Washington] was incapable of fear, meeting personal dangers with the calmest unconcern. Perhaps the strongest feature in his character was prudence, never acting until every circumstance, every consideration, was maturely weighed. His integrity was most pure, his justice the most inflexible I have ever known, no motives of interest or consanguinity, of friendship, or hatred, being able to bias his decision. He was, indeed, in every sense of the words, a wise, a good, and a great man.

THOMAS JEFFERSON

The people of this country are not jealous of fortunes, however great, which have been built up by honest development of great enterprises, which have been actually earned by business energy and sagacity; they are jealous only of speculative wealth, of the wealth which has been piled up by no effort at all, but only by shrewdness in playing on the credulity of others, taking advantage of the weakness of others, trading in the necessities of others. This is "predatory wealth."

WOODROW WILSON

When a man tells you that he got rich through hard work, ask him, "Whose?"

DON MARQUIS

She would have made a splendid wife, for crying only made her eyes more bright and tender.

O. HENRY

The wife of Willis Anderson came again to petition for his pardon. She hinted that her husband did not wish to be discharged from prison himself, and that it would be no relaxation of his punishment to turn him over to her.

JOHN QUINCY ADAMS

An ideal wife is any woman who has an ideal husband.

BOOTH TARKINGTON

You see, dear, it is not true that woman was made from man's rib; she was really made from his funny bone.

JAMES M. BARRIE

Women forgive injuries but never forget slights.

T. C. HALIBURTON

When a woman says, "They say," she means herself.

FRANK MCKINNEY HUBBARD

No woman ever hates a man for being in love with her, but many a woman hates a man for being a friend to her.

ALEXANDER POPE

Next to God, we are indebted to women, first for life itself,
and then for making it worth having.

A man's acts are usually right, but his reasons seldom are.

ELBERT HUBBARD

Bernard Shaw is an excellent man; he has not an enemy in
the world, and none of his friends like him.

OSCAR WILDE

I am bound to furnish my antagonists with arguments
but not with comprehension.

BENJAMIN DISRAELI

They are yet but ear-kissing arguments.

WILLIAM SHAKESPEARE

What I like in a good author is not what he says, but
what he whispers.

LOGAN PEARSALL

If the cattle are scattered, the tiger seizes them.

I am all kinds of a democrat, so far as I can discover—but the
root of the whole business is this, that I believe in the patriotism and energy and initiative of the average man.

WOODROW WILSON

None preaches better than the ant, and she says nothing.

BENJAMIN FRANKLIN

Two or more people getting together to write something
is like three people getting together to make a baby.

EVELYN WAUGH

Repartee is a duel fought with the points of jokes.

Every country has its beauty.

He that once deceives is ever suspected.

He did nothing in particular and did it very well.

W. S. GILBERT

When you open a door, do not forget to close it, and treat
your mouth the same way.

If a man dies and leaves his estate in an uncertain condition,
the lawyers become his heirs.

ED HOWE

Don't try to buy at the bottom and sell at the top.
This can't be done—except by liars.

BERNARD M. BARUCH

There is not better evidence than something written on paper.

I must complain the cards are ill-shuffled till
I have a good hand.

JONATHAN SWIFT

Gratitude is what shows whether a gift is appreciated.

I discarded a whole book because the leading character wasn't
on my wavelength. She was a lesbian with doubts
about her masculinity.

PETER DE VRIES

It's only common sense. If God wanted people to be gay,
He wouldn't have created Adam and Eve.
He would have created Adam and Steve.

ARTHUR HARMON

An idea isn't responsible for the people who believe in it.

DON MARQUIS

A good idea is one that not only gives the other fellow
a shot in the arm; it also makes him feel the needle
because he didn't think of it first.

He that knows little often repeats it.

Some men are born mediocre, some men achieve mediocrity,
and some men have mediocrity thrust upon them.

JOSEPH HELLER

It usually takes me more than three weeks to prepare
a good impromptu speech.

MARK TWAIN

Repression is the seed of revolution.

DANIEL WEBSTER

Animals are such agreeable friends—they ask no questions,
they pass no criticisms.

GEORGE ELIOT

I cannot live without books.

THOMAS JEFFERSON

Books are the bees which carry the quickening pollen from
one to another mind.

JAMES RUSSELL LOWELL

A home without books is like a kitchen without food.

How many a man has dated a new era in his life
from the reading of a book.

HENRY DAVID THOREAU

The desk is a dangerous place from which to watch the world.

JOHN LE CARRE

Football is, after all, a wonderful way to get rid of aggressions
without going to jail for it.

HEYWOOD HALE BROUN

The normal person living to age seventy has 613,200 hours
of life. This is too long a period not to have fun.

One way to get high blood pressure is to go mountain
climbing over molehills.

EARL WILSON

Unfaithfulness in the keeping of an appointment is an
act of clear dishonesty. You may as well borrow
a person's money as his time.

HORACE MANN

In the game of life, it's a good idea to have a few early losses,
which relieves you of the pressure of trying to
maintain an undefeated season.

BILL VAUGHAN

If you haven't struck oil in your first three minutes, stop boring!

GEORGE JESSEL

The claim that American women are downtrodden and
unfairly treated is the fraud of the century.

PHYLLIS SCHLAFLY

He can compress the most words into the smallest ideas
of any man I ever met.

ABRAHAM LINCOLN

Genius is the ability to reduce the complicated to the simple.

The more the words, the less the meaning, and how does that
profit anyone?

ECCLESIASTES 6:11

Soft words are hard arguments.

Reckless words pierce like
a sword, but the tongue of the wise brings healing.

PROVERBS 12:18

During a long life I have had to eat my own words many
times, and I have found it a very nourishing diet.

WINSTON CHURCHILL

There are three reasons for becoming a writer: The first is that
you need the money; the second that you have something to say
that you think the world should know; the third is that you
can't think what to do with the long winter evenings.

QUENTIN CRISP

If you want to be a writer—stop talking about it
and sit down and write!

JACKIE COLLINS

When I face the desolate impossibility of writing five hundred
pages, a sick sense of failure falls on me, and I know I can never
do it. This happens every time. Then gradually I write one page
and then another. One day's work is all I can permit myself to
contemplate, and I eliminate the possibility of ever finishing.

JOHN STEINBECK

Like most writers, I don't like to write;
I like to have written.

WILLIAM ZINSSER

I want to pay tribute to my four writers: Matthew,
Mark, Luke, and John.

BISHOP FULTON J. SHEEN

A poet who reads his verse in public may have
other nasty habits.

ROBERT HEINLEIN

He inquired of an old man whether it were sinful to write for
money. And the old man answered, "There be two kinds of
writers, my son: to wit, those who write for money and get it,
and those who write for money and don't get it."

T. W. H. CROSLAND

I don't want to be a doctor and live by men's diseases, nor a minister to live by their sins, nor a lawyer to live by their quarrels.
So I don't see there's anything left for me but to be an author.

NATHANIEL HAWTHORNE

The greatest part of a writer's time is spent
in reading, in order to write.
A man will turn over half a library
to make one book.

SAMUEL JOHNSON

I love being a writer.
What I can't stand is the paperwork.

PETER DE VRIES

The great struggle of a writer is to learn to write
as he would talk.

The profession of book writing makes horse racing seem like a
solid, stable business.

JOHN STEINBECK

Find a subject you care about and which you in your heart feel others should care about. It is the genuine caring, and not your games with language, which will be the most compelling and seductive element in your style.

KURT VONNEGUT

Make 'em laugh; make 'em cry; make 'em wait.

CHARLES READE

As a general rule, run your pen through every other word you have written; you have no idea what vigor it will give your style.

SYDNEY SMITH

The present letter is a very long one, simply because I had no leisure to make it shorter.

BLAISE PASCAL

Originality is nothing but judicious imitation. The most original writers borrowed one from another. The instruction we find in books is like fire. We fetch it from our neighbor's, kindle it at home, communicate it to others, and it becomes the property of all.

VOLTAIRE

The secret of all good writing is sound judgment.

HORACE

There is no subject so old that something new cannot be said about it.

FEODOR DOSTOEVSKI

You don't write because you want to say something; you write because you've got something to say.

F. SCOTT FITZGERALD

What is written without effort is in general read
without pleasure.

SAMUEL JOHNSON

Originality is the science of concealing your scores.

Vigorous writing is concise. A sentence should contain no
unnecessary words, a paragraph no unnecessary sentences, for
the same reason that a drawing should have no unnecessary
lines and a machine no unnecessary parts. This requires not that
the writer make all his sentences short, or that he avoid all
detail and treat his subjects only in outline, but that every word
tell.

WILLIAM STRUNK

Writing is easy. All you do is stare at a blank sheet of paper
until drops of blood form on your forehead.

GENE FOWLER

Write—if you find work.

BOB AND RAY

Why doth one man's yawning make another yawn?

ROBERT BURTON

The greater the cause, the greater the possibility for collision.

The best impromptu speeches are those written
well in advance.

RUTH GORDON

No man would listen to you talk if he didn't know it
was his turn next.

EDGAR WATSON HOWE

RESPONSIBILITY

One of the great sources of moral
and political breakdown in our day
is the reluctance of ordinary people
to accept responsibility.

W. T. PURKISER

I believe that every right implies a responsibility; every
opportunity, an obligation; every possession, a duty.

JOHN D. ROCKEFELLER JR.

When an archer misses the mark, he turns and looks for the
fault within himself. Failure to hit the bull's-eye is never the
fault of the target. To improve your aim, improve yourself.

GILBERT ARLAND

Hold yourself responsible for a higher standard
than anybody else expects of you.

HENRY WARD BEECHER

You must take responsibility for your own development.

Everyone is responsible for his own actions.

Anger is never without a reason, but seldom a good one.

BENJAMIN FRANKLIN

Anger makes dull men witty, but it keeps them poor.

FRANCIS BACON

Peace of mind is better than giving them a piece of your mind.

J. P. MCEVOY

Habit is like a soft bed—easy to get into, hard to get out of.

KELLY FORDYCE

Habit is a cable; we weave a thread of it every day, and at last we cannot break it.

HORACE MANN

It is easy to assume a habit; but when you try to cast it off, it will take skin and all.

HENRY W. SHAW

Habit is habit, and not to be flung out of the window by any man, but coaxed downstairs a step at a time.

MARK TWAIN

Nothing so needs reforming as other people's habits.

MARK TWAIN

We are creatures of habit. Any habit, good or bad, once formed is difficult to break. John Dryden once said, "Habits gather by unseen degrees, as brooks make rivers, rivers run to seas."

GUNDAR A. MYRAN

Habit is a shirt of iron.

Never go to bed mad. Stay up and fight.

PHYLLIS DILLER

An offended brother is more unyielding than a fortified city, and disputes are like the barred gates of a citadel.

PROVERBS 18:19

The size of a man can be measured by the size of the thing that makes him angry.

JOHN MORLEY

A DECALOGUE OF CANONS FOR OBSERVATION IN PRACTICAL LIFE

1. Never put off till tomorrow what you can do today.
2. Never trouble another for what you can do yourself.
3. Never spend your money before you have it.
4. Never buy what you do not want because it is cheap; it will be dear to you.
5. Pride costs us more than hunger, thirst, and cold.
6. We never repent of having eaten too little.
7. Nothing is troublesome that we do willingly.
8. How much pain have cost us the evils which have never happened.
9. Take things always by their smooth handle.
10. When angry, count to ten before you speak; if very angry, a hundred.

THOMAS JEFFERSON

1. You cannot bring about prosperity by discouraging thrift.
2. You cannot strengthen the weak by weakening the strong.
3. You cannot help small men up by tearing big men down.
4. You cannot help the poor by destroying the rich.
5. You cannot lift the wage-earner up by pulling the wage-payer down.
6. You cannot keep out of trouble by spending more than your income.
7. You cannot further the brotherhood of man by inciting class hatred.
8. You cannot establish sound social security on borrowed money.
9. You cannot build character and courage by taking away a man's initiative and independence.
10. You cannot help men permanently by doing for them what they could and should do for themselves.

ABRAHAM LINCOLN

Anger has no eyes.

Anger has no counsel.

Anger is the only thing to put off till tomorrow.

He who conquers his anger has conquered an enemy.

A little integrity is better than any career.

RALPH WALDO EMERSON

As the poet Dante once said, "The hottest places in hell
are reserved for those who, in a time of great moral crisis,
maintain their neutrality."

JOHN F. KENNEDY

Only those are fit to live who do not fear to die; and
none are fit to die who have shrunk from the joy of life and
the duty of life. Both life and death are parts
of the same great adventure.

THEODORE ROOSEVELT

God give us men! A time like this demands
Strong minds, great hearts, true faith, and ready hands.
Men whom the lust of office does not kill,
Men whom the spoils of office cannot buy,
Men who possess opinions and a will,
Men who have honor, men who will not lie.

JOSIAH G. HOLLAND

Take care of the minutes, and the hours will
take care of themselves.

Only a life lived for others is the life worthwhile.

ALBERT EINSTEIN

A Bible and a newspaper in every house, a good school
in every district—all studied and appreciated as they merit—
are the principal support of virtue, morality, and civil liberty.

BENJAMIN FRANKLIN

The man who goes alone can start today; but he who travels
with another must wait till that other is ready.

HENRY DAVID THOREAU

One of the most difficult things to do is to be as pleasant in
your own home as you are in the homes of others.

A professional is a man who can do his job when he doesn't
feel like it. An amateur is a man who can't do his job
when he does feel like it.

JAMES AGATE

A man is never so on trial as in the moment of
excessive good fortune.

LEW WALLACE

The best reformers the world has ever seen are those who
commence on themselves.

GEORGE BERNARD SHAW

The sting of a reproach is the truth of it.

BENJAMIN FRANKLIN

He who guards his lips guards his life, but he who speaks
rashly will come to ruin.

PROVERBS 15:5

A ship is often lost with all on board on account of one man.

Drawing on my fine command of language, I said nothing.

ROBERT BENCHLEY

Neither let us be slandered from our duty by false accusations against us, nor frightened from it by menaces of destruction to the government, nor of dungeons to ourselves. Let us have faith that right makes might, and in that faith let us to the end dare to do our duty as we understand it.

ABRAHAM LINCOLN

If you were to ask what is the hardest task in the world, you might think of some muscular feat, some acrobatic challenge, some chore to be done on the battlefield or the playing field. Actually, however, there is nothing which we find more arduous than saying, "I was wrong."

SUNSHINE MAGAZINE

The advantage of always following the straight and narrow path is you avoid all the traffic.

Like a bad tooth or a lame foot is reliance on the unfaithful in times of trouble.

PROVERBS 25:19

Give us clear vision that we may know where to stand and what to stand for—because unless we stand for something, we shall fall for anything.

MEGIDDO MESSAGE

In the battle of existence, talent is the punch; tact is the clever footwork.

WILSON MIZNER

TRUTH

Are we disposed to be of the number
of those who, having eyes, see not,
and having ears, hear not the things
which so nearly concern their temporal salvation? For my
part, whatever
anguish of spirit it might cost, I
am willing to know the whole truth,
to know the worst and to provide for it.

PATRICK HENRY

Sometimes the kindest thing you can do for a person is to tell
him a truth that will prove very painful. But in so doing, you
may have saved him from serious harm or even greater pain. In
a world such as ours, people must learn to "take it." A painless
world is not necessarily a good world.

SYLVANUS AND EVELYN DUVALL

From the cowardice that shrinks from new truth,
From the laziness that is content with half-truths,
From the arrogance that thinks it knows all truth,
O, God of Truth, deliver us.

PRAYER OF THE SCHOLAR

A truth that's told with bad intent
Beats all the lies you can invent.

WILLIAM BLAKE

I have discovered the art of fooling diplomats; I speak the
truth, and they never believe me.

BENSO DI VACOUR

Even truth gets drowned when gold comes to the surface.

Men occasionally stumble over the truth, but most of them
pick themselves up and hurry off as if nothing happened.

WINSTON CHURCHILL

As scarce as truth is, the supply has always been
in excess of the demand.

HENRY WHEELER SHAW

There is nothing so powerful as truth—and
often nothing so strange.

DANIEL WEBSTER

A man had rather have a hundred lies told to him than one
truth which he does not wish should be told.

SAMUEL JOHNSON

The truth doesn't hurt unless it ought to.

B. C. FORBES

Truth always lags behind, limping along on the arm of time.

BALTASAR GRACIAN

You'll never get mixed up if you simply tell the truth.
Then you don't have to remember what you have said, and
you never forget what you have said.

SAM RAYBURN

He who has the right needs not to fear . . . truth is generally
the best vindication against slander.

ABRAHAM LINCOLN

Half the truth is often a great lie.

BENJAMIN FRANKLIN

Who speaks the truth stabs falsehood to the heart.

JAMES RUSSELL LOWELL

Truth is tough. It will not break, like a bubble, at a touch; nay,
you may kick it about all day, like a football, and
it will be round and full at evening.

OLIVER WENDELL HOLMES JR.

Truthful lips endure forever, but a lying tongue
lasts only a moment.

PROVERBS 12:19

He who speaks the truth should have one foot in the stirrup.

Nothing is so burdensome as a secret.

It seems like one o' the hardest lessons t' be learned in this life
is where your business ends an' somebody else's begins.

FRANK MCKINNEY

A man that should call everything by its right name, would
hardly pass the streets without being knocked down
as a common enemy.

LORD HALIFAX

Some circumstantial evidence is very strong, as when
you find a trout in the milk.

HENRY DAVID THOREAU

Casting the lot settles disputes and keeps
strong opponents apart.

PROVERBS 18:18

The art of conversation is not knowing what you ought to say,
but what one ought not to say.

Craft must have clothes, but truth loves to go naked.

JONATHAN SWIFT

The most casual student of history knows that, as a matter of fact, truth does not necessarily vanquish. What is more, truth can never win unless it is promulgated. Truth does not carry within itself an antitoxin to falsehood. The cause of truth must be championed, and it must be championed dynamically.

WILLIAM F. BUCKLEY JR.

Honest criticism is hard to take, particularly from a relative, a friend, an acquaintance, or a stranger.

FRANKLIN P. JONES

Why is it that we rejoice at a birth and grieve at a funeral? It is because we are not the person involved.

MARK TWAIN

When death comes, the rich man has no money, the poor man no debt.

Debt is a bad companion.

He that gets out of debt grows rich.

One of the greatest disservices you can do a man is to lend him money that he can't pay back.

How many illustrious and noble heroes have lived too long by one day!

JEAN JACQUES ROUSSEAU

Nothing helps you to enjoy your job like an independent income.

Of all the freedoms a man may enjoy, none can quite match that which comes from being completely free of debt.

You can fool some of the people all of the time, and
all of the people some of the time, but
you cannot fool all the people all the time.

ABRAHAM LINCOLN

You may be sure that when a man begins to
call himself a realist he is preparing to do something
that he is secretly ashamed of doing.

SYDNEY J. HARRIS

Man learns little from victory, but much from defeat.

God's delays aren't necessarily His denials.

Desire has no rest.
The devil can quote Scripture.

The devil has a chapel wherever God has a church.

A disease known is half cured.

A house divided against itself cannot stand.

ABRAHAM LINCOLN

Physicians think they do a lot for a patient when
they give his disease a name.

IMMANUEL KANT

A rumor is something that goes in one ear and in another.

Eloquence is the ability to say the right thing
when you think of it.

He who is truthful may be the enemy of many.

Error is always more busy than truth.

HOSEA BALLOU

To admit errors sets one free as the truth always does.

HANS KUNG

Facts do not cease to exist because they are ignored.

FRANKLIN FIELD

Facts are stubborn things; and whatever may be our wishes,
our inclinations, or the dictates of our passions, they cannot
alter the state of facts and evidence.

JOHN ADAMS

Facts are your friends.

NORM DANIELS

Too much fear creates slavery.

If you're going to tell people the truth, make
them laugh, or they'll kill you.

BILLY WILDER

Whoever flatters his neighbor is spreading a net for his feet.

PROVERBS 29:5

It is difficult to trap an old fox.

When the fox is hungry, he pretends to be asleep.

The secret of getting along with others consists
in first mastering the art of getting along with yourself.

Men are like that—they can resist sound argument and
yield to a glance.

HONORÉ DE BALZAC

I respect faith but doubt is what gets you an education . . .
A good listener is not only popular everywhere but
after a while he knows something.

WILSON MIZNER

A good listener is one who can get you to tell him more than
you ever intended to.

If everyone thought alike, no goods would be sold.

He who is guilty is the one who has much to say.

The trouble with hindsight is that it usually improves your
vision and your envy at the same time.

Haste is the sister of repentance.

Now hatred is by far the longest pleasure; men love in haste,
but they detest at leisure.

LORD BYRON

If somebody throws a brick at me, I can catch it and
throw it back. But when somebody awards
a decoration to me, I am out of words.

HARRY S. TRUMAN

Great honors are great burdens.

If you can talk brilliantly about a problem, it can create the
consoling illusion that it has been mastered.

STANLEY KUBRICK

Moral indignation is in most cases 2 percent moral,
48 percent indignation and 50 percent envy.

VITTORIO DE SICA

There is no good in arguing with the inevitable.
The only argument available with an east wind is
to put on your overcoat.

JAMES RUSSELL LOWELL

No one can make you feel inferior without your consent.

ELEANOR ROOSEVELT

A stranger is someone with whom you feel strange.

BOB MANDEL

To have a grievance is to have a purpose in life.

ERIC HOFFER

To a woman there is something indescribably inviting
in a man whom other women favor.

HONORÉ DE BALZAC

We are all inclined to judge ourselves by our ideals; others
by their acts.

HAROLD NICOLSON

Never try to tell everything you know.
It may take too short a time.

NORMAN FORD

It often shows a fine command of language to say nothing.

A wise lawyer never goes to law himself.

I wanted to make it a law that only those lawyers and
attorneys should receive fees who had won their cases.
How much litigation would have been prevented
by such a measure!

NAPOLEON

Loan a man your ears and you will immediately open
a pathway to his heart.

It is more difficult, and calls for higher energies of soul, to
live a martyr than to die one.

HORACE MANN

The advantage of a bad memory is that one enjoys several
times the same good things for the first time.

FRIEDRICH W. NIETZSCHE

Men are nervous of remarkable women.

JAMES M. BARRIE

Nothing helps to stretch one's mind like a good idea
that you can get all excited about.

Great minds discuss ideas, average minds discuss events, small
minds discuss people.

All wrongdoing is done in the sincere belief that
it is the best thing to do.

ARNOLD BENNETT

A person seldom makes the same mistake twice.
Generally it's three times or more.

What loneliness is more lonely than mistrust.

GEORGE ELIOT

Modesty: the gentle art of enhancing your charm
by pretending not to be aware of it.

The mouth is easy to open but difficult to close.

He who steals a needle will steal an ox.

Most of us have never lived in normal times.

Literature is strewn with the wreckage of men who have
minded beyond reason the opinion of others.

VIRGINIA WOOLF

Better a pain in your heart than shame before men.

If you want to please everybody, you'll die before your time.

The highest price we can pay for anything, is to ask it.

W. S. LANDOR

A man apt to promise is apt to forget.

THOMAS FULLER

More trouble is caused in the world by indiscreet answers
than by indiscreet questions.

SYDNEY J. HARRIS

When public opinion changes, it is with the
rapidity of thought.

THOMAS JEFFERSON

Nations, like individuals, are subjected to punishments and
chastisements in this world.

ABRAHAM LINCOLN

No question is so difficult to answer as that to which
the answer is obvious.

GEORGE BERNARD SHAW

Next to the originator of a good sentence is the first quoter of it.

RALPH WALDO EMERSON

Every life is its own excuse for being, and to deny or refute the untrue things that are said of you is an error in judgment. All wrongs recoil upon the doer, and the man who makes wrong statements about others is himself to be pitied, not the man he vilifies. It is better to be lied about than to lie.

ELBERT HUBBARD

To know how to read is to light a lamp in the wind, to release the soul from prison, to open a gate to the universe.

PEARL BUCK

There is a great deal of difference between the eager man who wants to read a book and the tired man who wants a book to read.

G. K. CHESTERTON

The young are often full of revolt, and they're often pretty revolting about it.

Riches are gotten with pain, kept with care, and lost with grief.

What men value in this world is not rights but privileges.

H. L. MENCKEN

Put a rogue in the limelight, and he will act like an honest man.

NAPOLEON

Saints are not formed in great crises but in the ordinary grind of daily life.

EVERYDAY SAINT

Scandal is like an egg: When it is hatched, it has wings.

We are not satisfied to be right unless we can prove
others to be quite wrong.

JOHN W. HAZARD

To whom thy secret thou dost tell, to him
thy freedom thou dost sell.

BENJAMIN FRANKLIN

If you wish to preserve your secret, wrap it up in frankness.

ALEXANDER SMITH

A woman can keep one secret—the secret of her age.

VOLTAIRE

A secret stays long in darkness, but it will see the light.

To whom you tell your secret you surrender your freedom.

Secrets, after all, do serve a purpose. Those you tell them to
get so much pleasure out of telling them to somebody else.

A ship in harbor is safe, but that is not what ships are built for.

JOHN A. SHEDD

Speaking the truth in love may mean, at
times, keeping silence.

WILLARD L. SPERRY

Silence is one of the hardest arguments to refute.

JOSH BILLINGS

Silence: the unbearable repartee.

G. K. CHESTERTON

The most powerful single thing you can do to
have influence over others is to smile at them.

Sorrow will pay no debt.

If a thing goes without saying, let it.
JACOB M. BRAUDE

You may talk too much on the best of subjects.
BENJAMIN FRANKLIN

Think twice before you speak, and then say it to yourself.
ELBERT HUBBARD

Who speaks of the wolf sees his tail.

One advantage of thinking twice before you speak
is that you will speak seldom.

Most of our suspicions of others are aroused by
what we know of ourselves.

Swearing was invented as a compromise between
running away and fighting.
FINLEY PETER DUNNE

You do not swear at your serious troubles.
One only swears at trifling annoyances.
G. F. TURNER

Television is an invention that permits you to be
entertained in your living room by people
you wouldn't have in your home.
DAVID FROST

Two things a man should never be angry at: what
he can help, and what he cannot help.

No one can guard against treachery.

Never trust a man who speaks well of everybody.

CHURTON COLLINS

And when he is out of sight, quickly also is he out of mind.

THOMAS A. KEMPIS

The accomplice is as bad as the thief.

There are very few people who don't become more interesting
when they stop talking.

MARY LOWRY

We are inclined to believe those whom we do not know,
because they have never deceived us.

SAMUEL JOHNSON

None knows the weight of another's burden.

To say what you think will certainly damage you in society;
but a free tongue is worth more than a thousand invitations.

LOGAN PEARSALL SMITH

On an occasion of this kind, it becomes more than a moral
duty to speak one's mind. It becomes a pleasure.

OSCAR WILDE

Too many captains run the ship aground.

The world tolerates conceit from those who are successful, but
not from anybody else.

JOHN BLAKE

Confession is the first step to repentance.

It is easy to bid the devil be your guest, but
difficult to get rid of him.

It is error alone which needs the support of government.
Truth can stand by itself.

THOMAS JEFFERSON

He that rewards flattery begs it.

Thousands of geniuses live and die undiscovered—either
by themselves or by others.

MARK TWAIN

Next to ingratitude, the most painful thing to bear is gratitude.

HENRY WARD BEECHER

A life isn't significant except for its impact on other lives.

JACKIE ROBINSON

Even a liar tells a hundred truths to one lie; he
has to, to make the lie good for anything.

HENRY WARD BEECHER

Rudeness is the weak man's imitation of strength.

ERIC HOFFER

There is no spectacle on earth more appealing than
that of a beautiful woman in the act of cooking dinner
for someone she loves.

THOMAS WOLFE

Even a fool has one accomplishment.

If you play it safe in life, you've decided that you
don't want to grow anymore.

SHIRLEY HUFSTEDLER

Unless you try to do something beyond what you
already mastered, you will never grow.

RONALD OSBORN

When you're through changing, you're through.

BRUCE BARTON

Nothing is so exhausting as indecision, and
nothing is so futile.

BERTRAND RUSSELL

We judge ourselves by what we feel capable of doing, while
others judge us by what we have already done.

HENRY W. LONGFELLOW

People are lonely because they build walls instead of bridges.

JOSEPH F. NEWTON

If a man has good manners and is not afraid of other people,
he will get by even if he is stupid.

SIR DAVID ECCLES

We run ourselves down so as to be praised by others.

LA ROCHEFOUCAULD

I can live for two months on a good compliment.

MARK TWAIN

People seldom want to walk over you until you lie down.

ELMER WHEELER

There are few wild beasts more to be dreaded than a talking
man having nothing to say.

JONATHAN SWIFT

People support what they help to create.

WISDOM

Wisdom is knowledge that has been
cured in the brine of tears.

RICHARD ARMOUR

Though a man may become learned by another's learning, he
can never be wise but by his own wisdom.

MICHEL DE MONTAIGNE

Wisdom grows when knowledge is lived.

SIDNEY B. SIMON

Nine-tenths of wisdom consists in being wise in time.

THEODORE ROOSEVELT

The art of being wise is the art of knowing what to overlook.

WILLIAM JAMES

If a man had half as much foresight as he has twice as much
hindsight, he'd be a lot better off.

ROBERT J. BURDETTE

Pain makes man think. Thought makes man wise.
Wisdom makes life endurable.

JOHN PATRICK.

Be wiser than other people if you can, but do not tell them so.

LORD CHESTERFIELD

At a dinner party, one should eat wisely but not too well and
talk well but not too wisely.

W. SOMERSET MAUGHAM

It takes great wisdom to laugh at
one's own misfortunes.

A man is rich in proportion to the number of things he can
afford to let alone.

HENRY DAVID THOREAU

Many foxes grow gray, but few grow good.

BENJAMIN FRANKLIN

Be always a little afraid so that you never have
need of being much afraid.

The one part of the human anatomy that continues to grow
after twenty-one is the wishbone.

For many years now, you and I have been shushed like children
and told there are no simple answers to the complex problems
that are beyond our comprehension. Well, the truth is, there are
simple answers. There are just not easy ones.

RONALD REAGAN

To every answer you can find a new question.

Anticipation is often greater than realization.

R. E. PHILLIPS

When the beer goes in, the wits go out.

No man's credit is as good as his money.

HENRY VAN DYKE

A good way to get a boy to cut the grass is to forbid him to
touch the lawn mower.

Too many bricklayers make a lopsided house.
Some are very busy and yet do nothing.

I remember that a wise friend of mine did usually say, "That
which is everybody's business is nobody's business."

IZAAK WALTON

No matter how much care is taken, someone
will always be misled.

He who rejects change is the architect of decay.
The only human institution which rejects
progress is the cemetery.

HAROLD WILSON

All charming people have something to conceal, usually
their total dependence on the appreciation of others.

CYRIL CONNOLLY

Wildest colts make the best horses.

The secret of being able to take things as they come is
to stagger the unpleasant ones far enough apart.

BOOK OF COMMON PRAYER

The art of being a good guest is to know when to leave.

He that always complains is never pitied.

No great advance has ever been made in science, politics, or
religion, without controversy.

LYMAN BEECHER

If you have to eat crow, eat it while it's hot.

ALBEN BARKLEY

No man resolved to make the most of himself can spare time for personal contention. Still less can he afford to take all the consequences, including the vitiating of his temper, and the loss of self-control. Yield larger things to which you can show no more than equal right; and yield lesser ones, though clearly your own. Better give your path to a dog than be bitten by him in contesting for the right. Even killing the dog would not cure the bite.

ABRAHAM LINCOLN

The maxim of buying nothing without the money in our pocket to pay for it, would make of our country one of the happiest upon earth. Experience during the war proved this; as I think every man will remember that under all the privations it obliged him to submit to during that period he slept sounder and awaked happier than he can do now. Desperate of finding relief from a free course of justice, I look forward to the abolition of all credit as the only other remedy which can take place.

THOMAS JEFFERSON

Culture is only culture when the owner is not aware of its existence. Capture culture, hogtie it, and clap your brand upon it, and you did the shock that has killed the thing you loved. You can brand a steer, but you cannot brand deer.

ELBERT HUBBARD

Death softens all resentments, and the conscious of
a common inheritance of frailty and weakness
modifies the severity of judgment.

JOHN GREENLEAF WHITTIER

Desire will entice beyond the bounds of reason.

Let the devil get into the church, and he will mount the altar.

There is a healthful hardiness about real dignity that never dreads contact and communion with others, however humble.

WASHINGTON IRVING

Next to temperance, a quiet conscience, a cheerful mind, and active habits, I place early rising as a means of health and happiness.

TIMOTHY FLINT

The morning hour has gold in its mouth.

Perhaps an editor might begin a reformation in some such way as this. Divide his paper into four chapters, heading the first "Truths"; second, "Probabilities"; third, "Possibilities"; fourth, "Lies."

THOMAS JEFFERSON

Even though you become the enemy of a good man, don't become the friend of a bad man.

Better to be envied than pitied.

HERODOTUS

Nothing sharpens sight like envy.

Wise men learn by other men's mistakes, fools by their own.

H. G. BOHN

There are a thousand hacking at the branches of evil to one who is striking at the root.

HENRY DAVID THOREAU

The evolutionists seem to know everything about the missing link except the fact that it is missing.

G. K. CHESTERTON

I wish no explanation made to our enemies.
What they want is a squabble and a fuss, and that they can
have if we explain, and they cannot have if we don't.

ABRAHAM LINCOLN

One eye of the master's sees more than ten of the servants'.

People in general will much better bear being told of their
vices and crimes than of their failings and weaknesses.

LORD CHESTERFIELD

The eyes are the mirror of the soul.

Don't tell your friends their social faults; they will
cure the fault and never forgive you.

LOGAN PEARSALL SMITH

Nothing is so great an instance of ill manners as flattery.
If you flatter all the company, you please none; if you
flatter only one or two, you affront the rest.

JONATHAN SWIFT

Never confuse activity, talk, or money with genius.

Gold begets in brethren hate;
Gold in families, debate;
Gold does friendship separate;
Gold does civil wars create.

ABRAHAM COWLE

Nothing improves a person's hearing like overhearing.

If you live with your ear to the ground, you will hear many
things which your feet would have trampled over.

Do not make friends with a hot-tempered man, do not
associate with one easily angered, or you may learn
his ways and get yourself ensnared.

PROVERBS 22:24-25

There's nothing really consistent about human behavior
except its tendency to drift toward evil.

A bad man is worse when he pretends to be a saint.

FRANCIS BACON

There are only two or three human stories, and
they go on repeating themselves as fiercely as if they had
never happened before.

WILLA CATHER

The maker of idols does not worship them.

One moment of patience may ward off great disaster; one
moment of impatience may ruin a whole life.

CHINESE WISDOM

An individual, thinking himself injured, makes
more noise than a state.

THOMAS JEFFERSON

A lawyer's ink writes nothing until you have
thrown silver into it.

The voice of the intelligence . . . is drowned out by the roar of
fear. It is ignored by the voice of desire. It is contradicted by the
voice of shame. It is hissed away by hate and extinguished by
anger. Most of all it is silenced by ignorance.

KARL MENNINGER

One day a farmer came to pay his rent to a man whose love of money was very great. After settling the account, the farmer said, "I will give you a shilling if you will let me go down to the vault and have a look at your money." The farmer was permitted to see the piles of gold and silver in the miser's big chest. After gazing for a while the farmer said, "Now I am as well-off as you are." "How can that be?" asked the man. "Why, sir" said the farmer, "you never use any of this money. All you do with it is look at it. I have looked at it, too, so I am just as rich as you are."

NEW CENTURY LEADER

Like Aesop's fox, when he had lost his tail, he would have all his fellow foxes cut off theirs.

ROBERT BURTON

Anger is cruel and fury overwhelming, but who can stand before jealousy?

PROVERBS 27:4

What does the LORD require of you? To act justly and to love mercy and to walk humbly with your God.

MICAH 6:8

Distrust all in whom the impulse to punish is powerful.

FRIEDRICH W. NIETZSCHE

What you have seen with your eyes do not bring hastily to court, for what will you do in the end if your neighbor puts you to shame? If you argue your case with a neighbor, do not betray another man's confidence, or he who hears it may shame you and you will never lose your bad reputation.

PROVERBS 25:7-10

Lend never that thing you need most.

If you find a leopard in your house, make him your friend.

And you experts in the law, woe to you, because you
load people down with burdens they can hardly carry, and
you yourselves will not lift one finger to help them.

LUKE 11:46

Be courteous to all but intimate with few, and let those few be
well-tried before you give them your confidence.

GEORGE WASHINGTON

There is no worse lie than a truth misunderstood by
those who hear it.

WILLIAM JAMES

A lie always needs a truth for a handle to it.
The worst lies are those whose blade is false, but
whose handle is true.

HENRY WARD BEECHER

Like a madman shooting firebrands or deadly arrows is a man
who deceives his neighbor and says, "I was only joking!"

PROVERBS 26:18-19

Discourage litigation. Persuade your neighbors to
compromise whenever you can.

ABRAHAM LINCOLN

But little-minded people's thoughts move in such a
small circle that five minutes' conversation gives you an arc
long enough to determine their whole curve.

OLIVER WENDELL HOLMES

When you fight a monster, beware lest you become a monster.

FRIEDRICH NIETZSCHE

Language has created the word "loneliness" to express
the pain of being alone, and the word "solitude" to express
the glory of being alone

PAUL TILLICH

I shall do nothing in malice.
What I deal with is too vast for malicious dealing.

ABRAHAM LINCOLN

Who is wise? He that learns from everyone.
Who is powerful? He that governs his passions.
Who is rich? He that is content.
Who is that? Nobody.

BENJAMIN FRANKLIN

Silence is not always tact and it is tact that is golden, not silence.

SAMUEL BUTLER

Men are men before they are lawyers or physicians or merchants
or manufacturers; and if you make them capable and sensible
men, they will make themselves capable and sensible lawyers or
physicians.

JOHN STUART MILL

Every man is an island, and often you row around and
around before you find a place to land.

HARRY EMERSON FOSDICK

I am more and more convinced that man is a dangerous creature and that power, whether vested in many or a few, is ever
grasping and like the grave, cries, "Give, give."

ABIGAIL ADAMS

For every one hundred men who can withstand adversity,
there is only one who can withstand prosperity.

THOMAS CARLYLE

Better to live on a corner of the roof than share a
house with a quarrelsome wife.

PROVERBS 25:24

As charcoal to embers and as wood to fire, so is a quarrelsome
man for kindling strife.

PROVERBS 26:21

He who knows the road can ride full trot.

There's small revenge in words, but words
may be greatly revenged.

BENJAMIN FRANKLIN

A thought, a sword, and a spade should never
be allowed to rust.

IRISH PROVERB

It seems as if I've been doing the same things since I was six
years old. I'm a few inches taller, and I have a graying beard,
but otherwise there's not much difference.

MAURICE SENDAK

Nothing is easier than self-deceit. For what each man wishes,
that he also believes to be true.

DEMOSTHENES

Sometimes you have to be silent to be heard.

STANISLAW J. LEC

A slander is like a hornet; if you cannot kill it dead at
the first blow, better not strike at it.

HENRY WHEELER SHAW

If you don't say anything, you won't be called on to repeat it.

CALVIN COOLIDGE

We better know there is fire whence we see much smoke rising than we could know it by one or two witnesses swearing to it. The witnesses may commit perjury, but the smoke cannot.

ABRAHAM LINCOLN

If you know how to spend less than you get, you have the philosopher's stone.

BENJAMIN FRANKLIN

The sublime and the ridiculous are often so nearly related, that it is difficult to class them separately. One step below the sublime, makes the ridiculous; and one step more above the ridiculous, makes the sublime again.

THOMAS PAINE

The tongue has the power of life and death, and those who love it will eat its fruit.

PROVERBS 18:21

He who guards his mouth and his tongue keeps himself from calamity.

PROVERBS 21:23

I long to accomplish a great and noble task, but it is my chief duty to accomplish humble tasks as though they are great and noble. The world is moved along, not only by the mighty shoves of its heroes, but also by the aggregate of the tiny pushes of each honest worker.

HELEN KELLER

There's no quicker way of cooking your goose than by letting your temper boil over.

Take your thoughts to bed with you, for the morning is wiser than the evening.

Lost, yesterday, somewhere between sunrise and sunset, two golden hours, each set with sixty diamond minutes. No reward is offered, for they are gone forever.

HORACE MANN

Dost thou love life? Then do not squander time, for that is the stuff life is made of.

BENJAMIN FRANKLIN

If we lose our money, it gives us some concern. If we are cheated or robbed of it, we are angry. But money lost may be found; what we are robbed of may be restored. The treasure of time, once lost, can never be recovered; yet we squander it as though it were nothing worth or we had no use of it.

BENJAMIN FRANKLIN

Time is the herb that cures all diseases.

BENJAMIN FRANKLIN

Time, like a snowflake, disappears while we're trying to decide what to do with it.

Towers are measured by their shadows, great men by those who speak evil of them.

It is time to fear when tyrants seem to kiss.

What we obtain too cheap, we esteem too lightly; 'tis dearness only that gives everything its value.

THOMAS PAINE

War with your vices, at peace with your neighbors, and let New Year find you a better man.

BENJAMIN FRANKLIN

Seldom set foot in your neighbor's house—too
much of you, and he will hate you.

PROVERBS 25:17

Do not wear yourself out to get rich; have the wisdom
to show restraint. Cast but a glance at riches, and
they are gone, for they will surely sprout wings and
fly off to the sky like an eagle.

PROVERBS 25:4-5

Water never rises above its level.

We never know the worth of water till the well is dry.

No one means all he says, and yet very few say all they mean,
for words are slippery and thought is viscous.

HENRY ADAMS

Words that come from the heart enter the heart.

An ill wound, but not an ill name, may be healed.

BENJAMIN FRANKLIN

Appear always what you are and a little less.

A man never tells you anything until you contradict him.

Though the bird may fly over your head, let
it not make its nest in your hair.

Too many boatmen will row the boat up the mountain.

What you can't communicate runs your life.

ROBERT ANTHONY

Everywhere I have sought rest and found it not except sitting
apart in a nook with a little book.

THOMAS A. KEMPIS

If we encountered a man of rare intellect, we
should ask him what books he read.

RALPH WALDO EMERSON

No corn without chaff.

Better inside a cottage than outside a castle.

Life is not so short but that there is alway
time enough for courtesy.

RALPH WALDO EMERSON

When all sins grow old, covetousness is young.

Ridicule is the deadliest of weapons against a lofty cause.

SAMUEL HOPKINS ADAMS

Let minor differences and personal preferences, if
there be such, go to the winds.

ABRAHAM LINCOLN

Since excuses were invented, no one is ever in the wrong.

Denying a fault doubles it.

Be careful what you set your heart upon—for
it will surely be yours.

JAMES BALDWIN

The best and most beautiful things in the world cannot be
seen or even touched. They must be felt with the heart.

HELEN KELLER

There are two faults in conversation, which appear very different, yet arise from the same root, and are equally blamable; I mean an impatience to interrupt others and the uneasiness of being interrupted ourselves.

JONATHAN SWIFT

A man's personal defects will commonly have, with the rest of the world, precisely that importance which they have to himself. If he makes light of them, so will other men.

RALPH WALDO EMERSON

He has a good judgment that relies not wholly on his own.

The heart is deceitful above all things and beyond cure. Who can understand it?

JEREMIAH 17:9

When you paint a dragon, you paint his skin; it is difficult to paint the bones. When you know a man, you know his face but not his heart.

A man's wisdom gives him patience; it is to his glory to overlook an offense.

PROVERBS 19:11

Life is what happens while you are making other plans.

The hardest job kids face today is learning good manners without seeing any.

FRED ASTAIRE

The richest man, whatever his lot, is he who's content with what he has got.

Though the bear be gentle, don't bite him by the nose.

THOMAS D'URFEY

War talk by men who have been in a war is
always interesting; whereas moon talk by a poet who
has not been on the moon is likely to be dull.

MARK TWAIN

The crucible for silver and the furnace for gold, but
man is tested by the praise he receives.

PROVERBS 27:21

Enough research will tend to support your theory.

A. BLOCK

Suspicion is far more apt to be wrong than right; oftener
unjust than just. It is no friend to virtue and
always an enemy to happiness.

HOSEA BALLOU

Of making many books there is no end, and
much study wearies the body.

ECCLESIASTES 12:12

Like a gold ring in a pig's snout is a beautiful woman who
shows no discretion.

PROVERBS 11:22

Do not fear when your enemies criticize you.
Beware when they applaud.

VO DONG GIANG

There is great force hidden in a sweet command.

Do not waste your high-energy hours. Invest them where they
yield the highest payoff.

Most powerful is he who has himself in his power.

SENECA

Life is a two-stage rocket. The first is physical energy—it ignites, and we are off. As physical energy diminishes, the spiritual stage must ignite to boost us into orbit, or we will fall back or plateau.

W. F. SMITH

Learning is acquired by reading books, but the much more necessary learning, the knowledge of the world, is only to be acquired by reading men and studying all the various facets of them.

LORD CHESTERFIELD

The first and most important step in improving
the utilization of your time is planning.

Great men are little men expanded; great lives are
ordinary lives intensified.

WILFRED A. PETERSON

If a man is fortunate, he will, before he dies, gather up as
much as he can of his civilized heritage and
transmit it to his children.

WILL DURANT

If men are so wicked (as we see them now) with religion, what
would they be without it?

The most valuable thing I have or ever expect to have is
enthusiasm, and I would rather pass this on to my children
than anything else.

WORK

As a remedy against all ills—poverty,
sickness, and melancholy—only one
thing is absolutely necessary:
a liking for work.

CHARLES BAUDELAIRE

I would rather have one man with enthusiasm working with
me than ten who are complacent.

Next to getting enthusiastic about your job, the
most important requirement to getting ahead is to become
enthusiastic about your boss.

Almost anyone can develop enthusiasm—but
the kind of enthusiasm that will get you somewhere is the
kind that possesses you!

I never did anything worth doing by accident, nor did any of
my inventions come by accident; they came by work.

THOMAS EDISON

A plowman on his legs is higher than a gentleman
on his knees.

BENJAMIN FRANKLIN

Do not waste a minute . . . not a second . . . in trying to
demonstrate to others the merits of your performance. If your
work does not indicate yourself, you cannot vindicate it.

THOMAS W. HIGGINSON

Work is difficult; that's why it's called work.

DAVID BROWN

A man's health seldom suffers from the work he loves
and does for its own sake.

HONORÉ DE BALZAC

Anyone can do any amount of work, provided it isn't the work
he is supposed to be doing at that moment.

ROBERT BENCHLEY

I like work; it fascinates me. I can sit and look at it for hours.
I love to keep it by me; the idea of getting rid of it
nearly breaks my heart.

JEROME K. JEROME

Work expands so as to fill the time available for its completion.

C. NORTHCOTE PARKINSON

The most unhappy of all men is the man who cannot tell what
he is going to do, who has got no work cut out for him in the
world, and does not go into it. For work is the grand cure for all
the maladies and miseries that ever beset mankind—honest
work, which you intend getting done.

THOMAS CARLYLE

When your work speaks for itself, don't interrupt.

HENRY J. KAISER

Work as if you were to live one hundred years;
Pray as if you were to die tomorrow.

BENJAMIN FRANKLIN

There is no substitute for hard work.

THOMAS EDISON

Nothing ever comes to one, that is worth having, except
as a result of hard work.

BOOKER T. WASHINGTON

The lady-bearer of this says she has two sons who want to work.
Set them at it, if possible. Wanting to work is so rare a merit
that it should be encouraged.

ABRAHAM LINCOLN

Where there are no oxen, the manger is empty, but from the
strength of an ox comes an abundant harvest.

PROVERBS 14:4

All hard work brings a profit, but mere talk
leads only to poverty.

PROVERBS 14:23

Fine work is its own flattery.

Hard work never killed anyone.

He who likes his work, to him work comes easy.

Fellows who roll up their sleeves seldom lose their shirts.

You cannot define talent.
All you can do is build the greenhouse and see if it grows.

WILLIAM P. STEVEN

Do your job and demand your compensation—
but in that order.

CARY GRANT

Activity is contagious.

RALPH WALDO EMERSON

Farming looks mighty easy when your plow is a pencil, and
you're a thousand miles from the cornfield.

DWIGHT D. EISENHOWER

With a good conscience our only sure reward, with history the final judge of our deeds, let us go forth to lead the land we love, asking His blessing and His help, but knowing that here on earth God's work must truly be our own.

JOHN F. KENNEDY

When you cease to make a contribution, you begin to die.

ELEANOR ROOSEVELT

Earth here is so kind, that just tickle her with a hoe and she laughs with a harvest.

DOUGLAS JERROLD

Genius is 1 percent inspiration and 99 percent perspiration.

THOMAS EDISON

The main difference between a genius and the average man in the same profession is that the genius doesn't go to bed until he is a lot more tired.

He who is fed by another's hand seldom gets enough.

If the hand would do what the tongue says, there would be no poverty.

Too many people who are looking for a helping hand don't even try to lift one of their own fingers.

"What is life's heaviest burden?" asked a youth of a sad and lonely old man. "To have nothing to carry," he answered.

E. SCOTT O'CONNOR

Scientists have not yet found a better way of putting flavor into food than a five-mile hike before dinner.

At the workingman's house, hunger looks in
but dares not enter.

Everything comes to him who hustles while he waits.

THOMAS EDISON

Things may come to those who wait, but only
the things left by those who hustle.

ABRAHAM LINCOLN

There is no kind of idleness by which we are so easily seduced
as that which dignifies itself by the appearance of business.

SAMUEL JOHNSON

Iron rusts from disuse; stagnant water loses its purity and in
cold weather becomes frozen; even so does inaction sap the
vigors of the mind.

LEONARDO DA VINCI

What is used, develops, and what is left unused,
atrophies, or wastes away.

No one is so busy as the man who has nothing to do.

FRENCH PROVERB

The best inheritance a parent can leave a child
is a will to work.

HIPPOCRATES

To get a job well done, assign it to the man who has the most
to lose, not to one who has everything to gain.

The trouble with many people today is that the only time they
are lost for something to do is when they are on the job.

One of the first things a person must do to climb the ladder of success is to take his hands out of his pockets.

He that riseth late must trot all day, and shall scarce overtake his business by night.

BENJAMIN FRANKLIN

If it weren't for the last minute, nothing would get done.

As a door turns on its hinges, so a sluggard turns on his bed.

PROVERBS 26:14

The sluggard craves and gets nothing, but the desires of the diligent are fully satisfied.

PROVERBS 13:4

One who is slack in his work is brother to one who destroys.

PROVERBS 18:9

Laziness travels so slowly that poverty soon overtakes him.

BENJAMIN FRANKLIN

A lazy boy and a warm bed are difficult to part.

Lead in the seat of one's pants will never turn to gold.

Thunder is good, thunder is impressive; but it is lightning that does the work.

MARK TWAIN

Luck really is a charitable thing—note how frequently it visits people who work the hardest.

Luck is what happens when preparation meets opportunity.

Perhaps the most damaging form of personal rejection is to tell a man there is nothing in the world for him to do. For worklessness equals meaninglessness; and meaninglessness eats at the foundation of all law, all morality, all joy in human relationships.

TIMOTHY L. SMITH

The lazy man is not ashamed of begging.

One of the surest ways to enjoy money is
to earn it before you spend it.

If you don't climb the high mountain, you can't
view the plain.

It's more painful to do nothing than something.

He that pays beforehand shall have his work ill done.

To work without payment is better than sitting idle.

People may get tireder by standing still than by going on.

Those who pray for a million dollars would get better results if
they prayed for a strong back and a good pair of hands.

I believe, I have always believed, and I will always believe
in private enterprise as the backbone of economic
well-being in America.

FRANKLIN D. ROOSEVELT

The best eraser in the world is an eight-hour dose of hard work.

Men are made stronger on realization that the helping hand
they need is at the end of their own right arm.

SIDNEY PHILLIPS

Property is the fruit of labor; property is desirable, is a positive good in the world. That some should be rich shows that others may become rich, and hence is just encouragement to industry and enterprise. Let not him who is houseless pull down the house of another, but let him work diligently and build one for himself, thus by example assuring that his own shall be safe from violence when built.

ABRAHAM LINCOLN

Doing for people what they can and ought to do for themselves is a dangerous experiment. In the last analysis, the welfare of the workers depends upon their own initiative. Whatever is done under the guise of philanthropy or social morality which in any way lessens initiative is the greatest crime that can be committed against the toilers. Let social busybodies and professional "public morals experts" in their fads reflect upon the perils they rashly invite under this pretense of social welfare.

SAMUEL GOMPERS

The winter asks you what you have done during the summer.

Nothing breeds fatigue like inactivity.

Opportunities are usually disguised as hard work, so most people don't recognize them.

ANN LANDERS

Of all the tonics devised by man, none is as stimulating as a good day's work.

Even though you're on the right track . . . you'll get run over if you just sit there.

WILL ROGERS

There has never yet been a man in our history who led a life
of ease whose name is worth remembering.

THEODORE ROOSEVELT

As a cure for worrying, work is better than whiskey.

THOMAS EDISON

The reason worry kills more people than work is that more
people worry than work.

The surest way to hold onto your shirt is to
roll up your sleeves.

Plow deep while sluggards sleep,
And you shall have corn to sell and to keep.

BENJAMIN FRANKLIN

Never fear the want of business. A man who qualifies himself
well for his calling, never fails of employment in it.

THOMAS JEFFERSON

HOWARD G. HENDRICKS

(Th.M., Dallas Theological Seminary; D.D., Wheaton College) is a distinguished professor and lecturer at Dallas Theological Seminary. He is also chairman of the Center for Christian Leadership. Dr. Hendricks has written or edited numerous books including *Heaven Help the Home*, *Teaching to Change Lives*, and *Husbands and Wives*. Howard Hendricks and his wife, Jeanne, have four children.

BOB PHILLIPS

holds a Ph.D. in counseling and is a licensed family counselor in the state of California. He is formerly the director of the Northwest Counseling Center, Fresno, California. He is presently the Executive Director of Hume Lake Christian Camps, one of America's largest youth camping programs.

Dr. Phillips has written more than fifty books with over four million copies in print.